WHAT YOU NEED

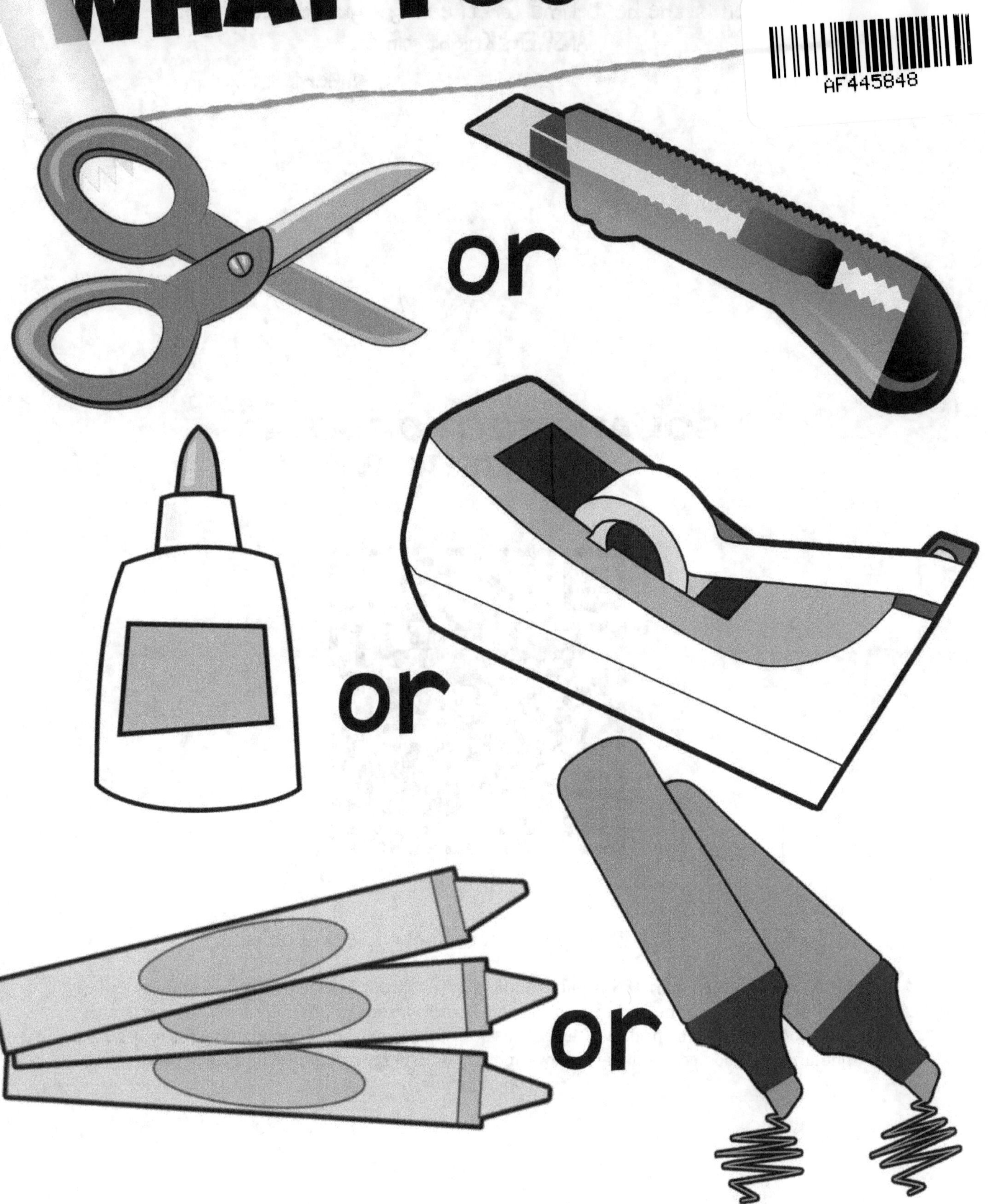

When is the best time for the king's guards to sleep?
ANSWER; Knight time

-Albert B. Squid

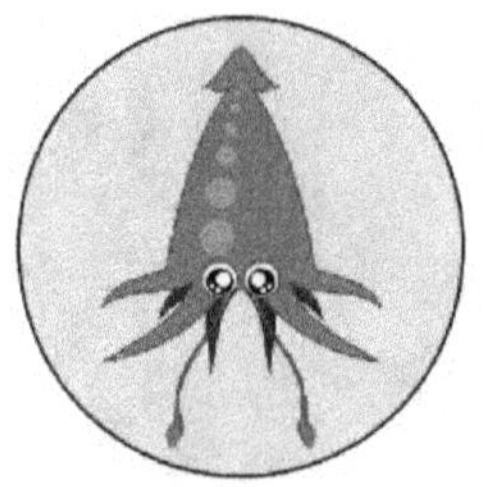

SQUARE ROOT OF SQUID PUBLISHING

HEY CASTLE BUILDER!!!

Are you ready to learn how a medieval castle was built? First, let's just say that there is no single blueprint for building a castle. Each castle design came about because of many different things (which we will get into on the following pages), but they do share some common things and we will learn what they are while actually building a paper model of a castle. So, if you are ready castle builder, **LET'S GET TO IT!!!**

CASTLE PARTS

MACHICOLATION- An overhang at the top of the curtain wall to drop flaming rocks covered in pig fat on an attacker.

BAILEY- The castle's courtyard.

CURTAIN WALL- The outside walls between corner towers.

KEEP- The castle's main tower and most protected building.

POSTERN- A secret door that led to the outside.

CORNER TOWER- The towers at each corner of the castle's curtain walls that are used to defend from attackers.

CRENEL- The opening notch at the top of roofs and curtain walls to allow for arrows to be shot.

MERLON- The opposite of the crenel. This is a block of stone to protect a guard from arrows.

BARBICAN- The front part of the gatehouse of a castle.

MURDER HOLE- These were holes in the ceilings and walls of the barbican that arrows could be shot through to injure an attacker.

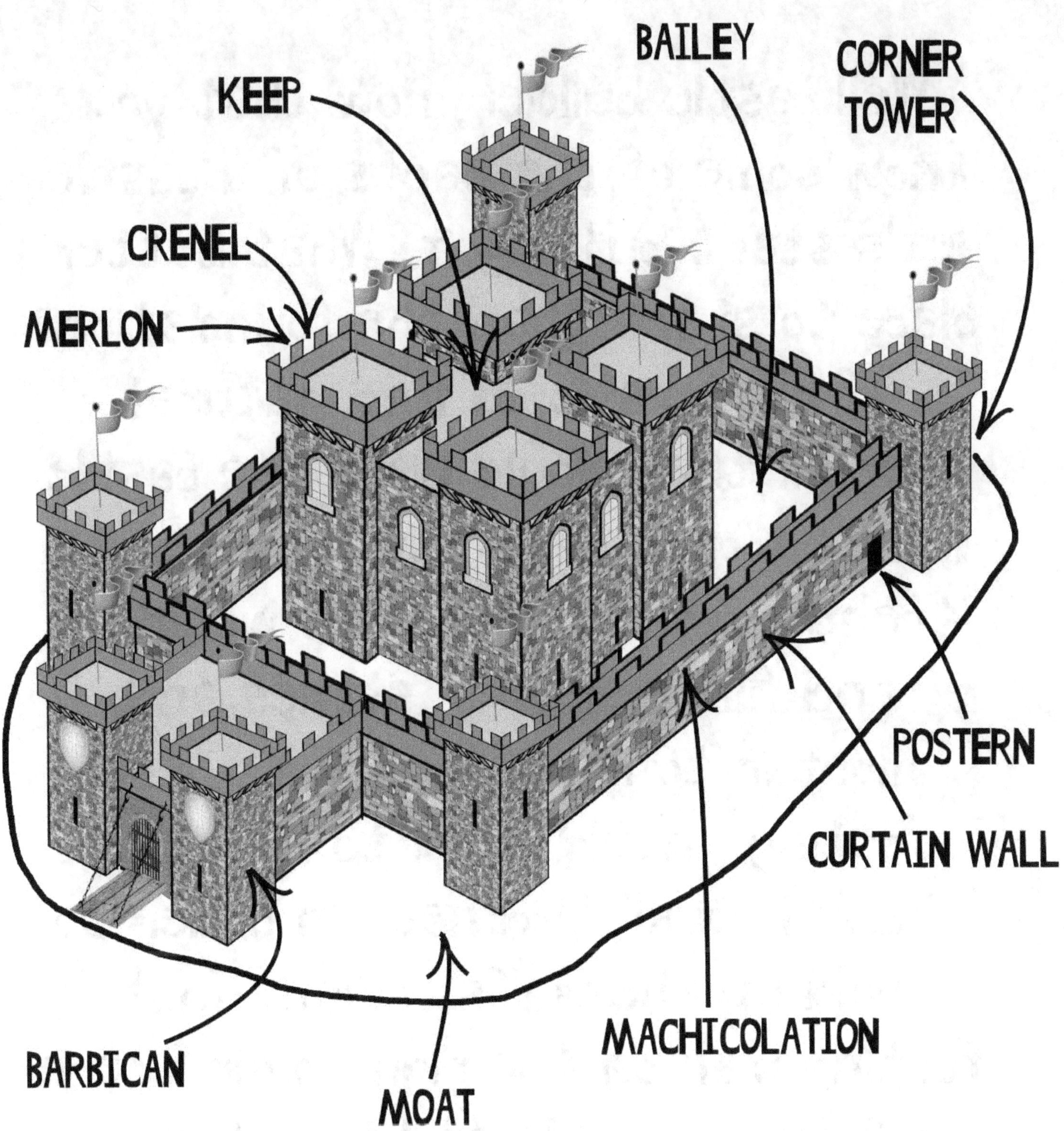

KEEP
BAILEY
CORNER TOWER
CRENEL
MERLON
POSTERN
CURTAIN WALL
MACHICOLATION
BARBICAN
MOAT

LET'S BUILD IT!!!

Well castle builder, now that you know some of the parts of a castle let's start building it. What better place to start than the foundation?

If builders could find natural bedrock they would build the castle walls on that, if not they would dig trenches where the walls would go and fill them with stones and mortar to make footings. These footings would need to be wider than the wall thickness in order to hold up the wall's weight. That footing plan on the right over there will be our guide and foundation upon which to build our paper castle.

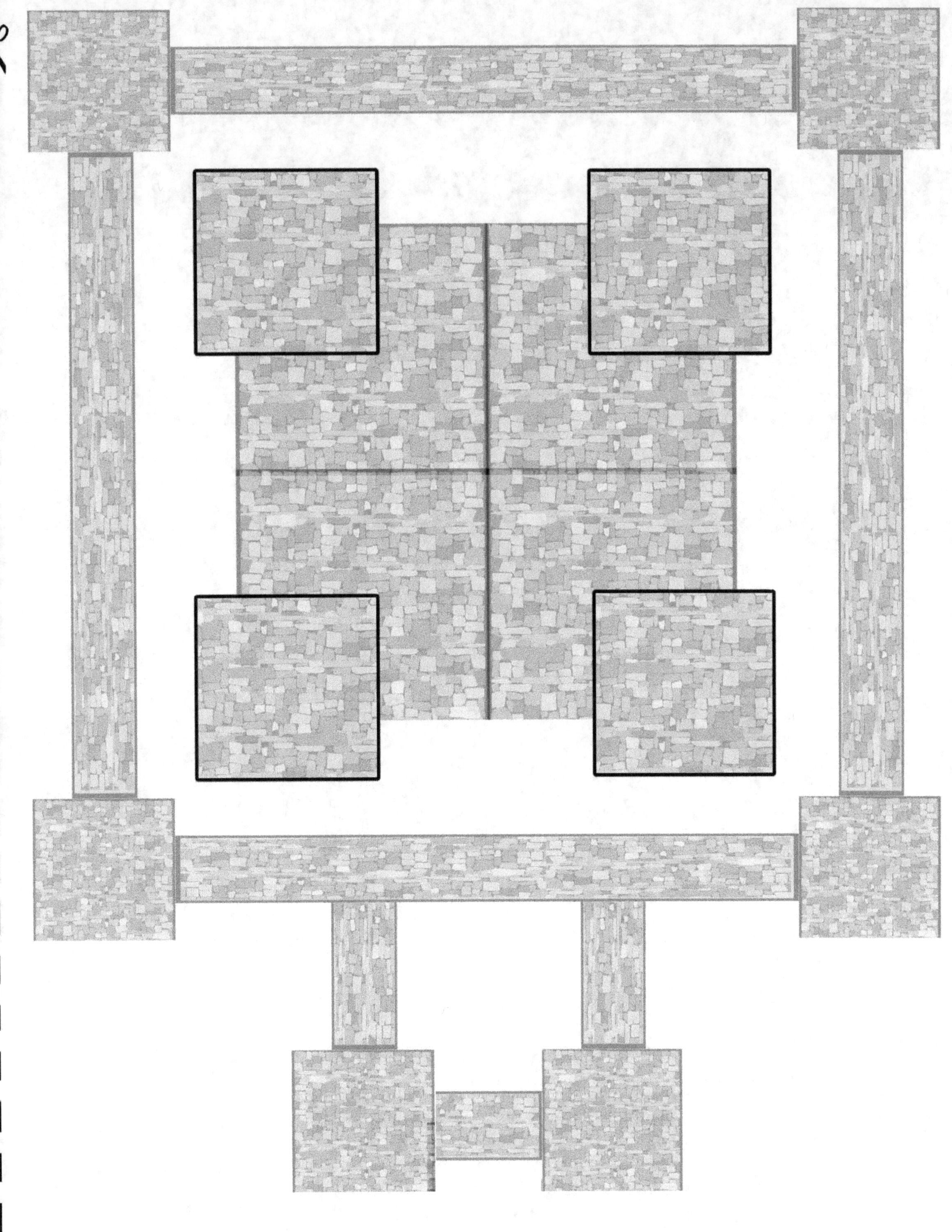

Find a piece of cardboard, cut it into a square, and glue the foundation plan to it. (Hint: You could even use the back cover of this book as a base if nothing else is available.)

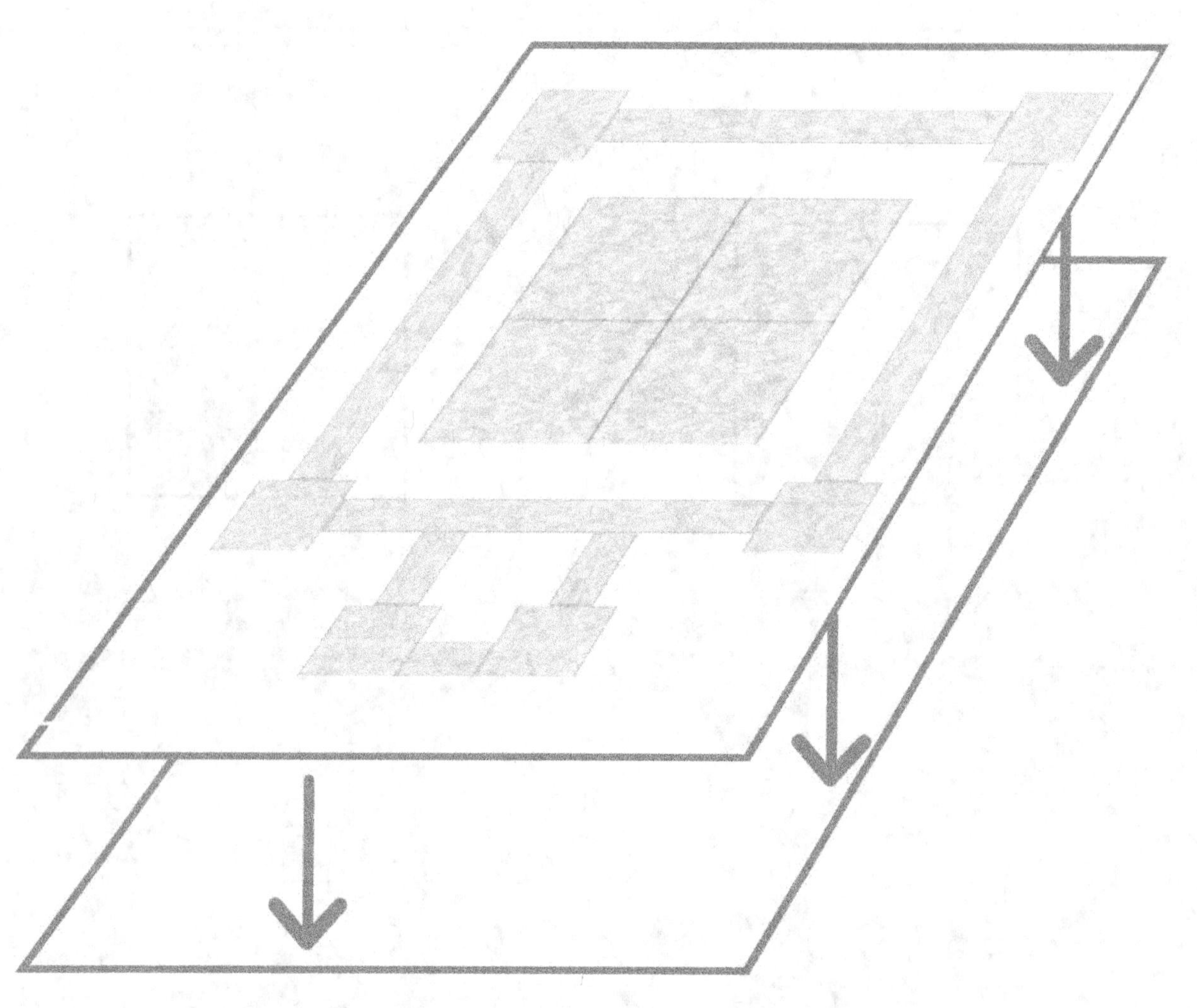

(this is the bottom side)

CORNER TOWERS

Well, you guessed it castle builder the corner towers were at the corners of the castle. Each tower was usually the first line of defense for a castle. These towers were connected with curtain walls (we'll get into those soon enough), and would have rooms to store weapons and other supplies along with guard stations which had small slits in the walls to allow guards to shoot arrows through without being hit by arrows themselves. When the medieval castle started appearing these towers were made of wood and square in shape. To make them stronger, Lords and Kings started making them with thick stone walls on the outside with stone vaults or wooden beams held up by corbels to make the interior floors. The square shape slowly started evolving into a round shape because attacking dudes figured out how to dig under the square ones and knock down the towers. Round towers were harder to undermine.

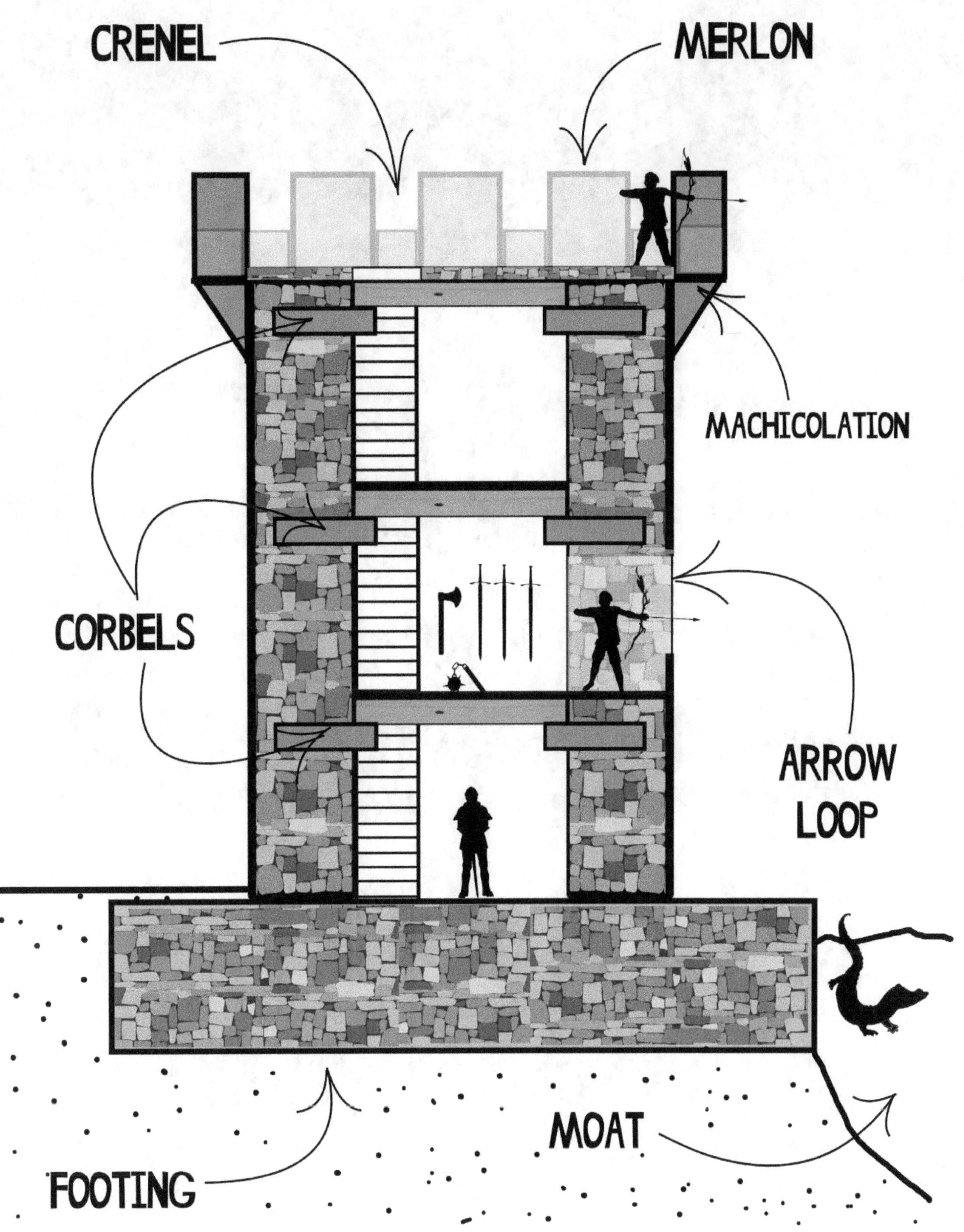

CRENEL
MERLON
MACHICOLATION
CORBELS
ARROW
LOOP
FOOTING
MOAT

SAVE THE SCRAP PAPER

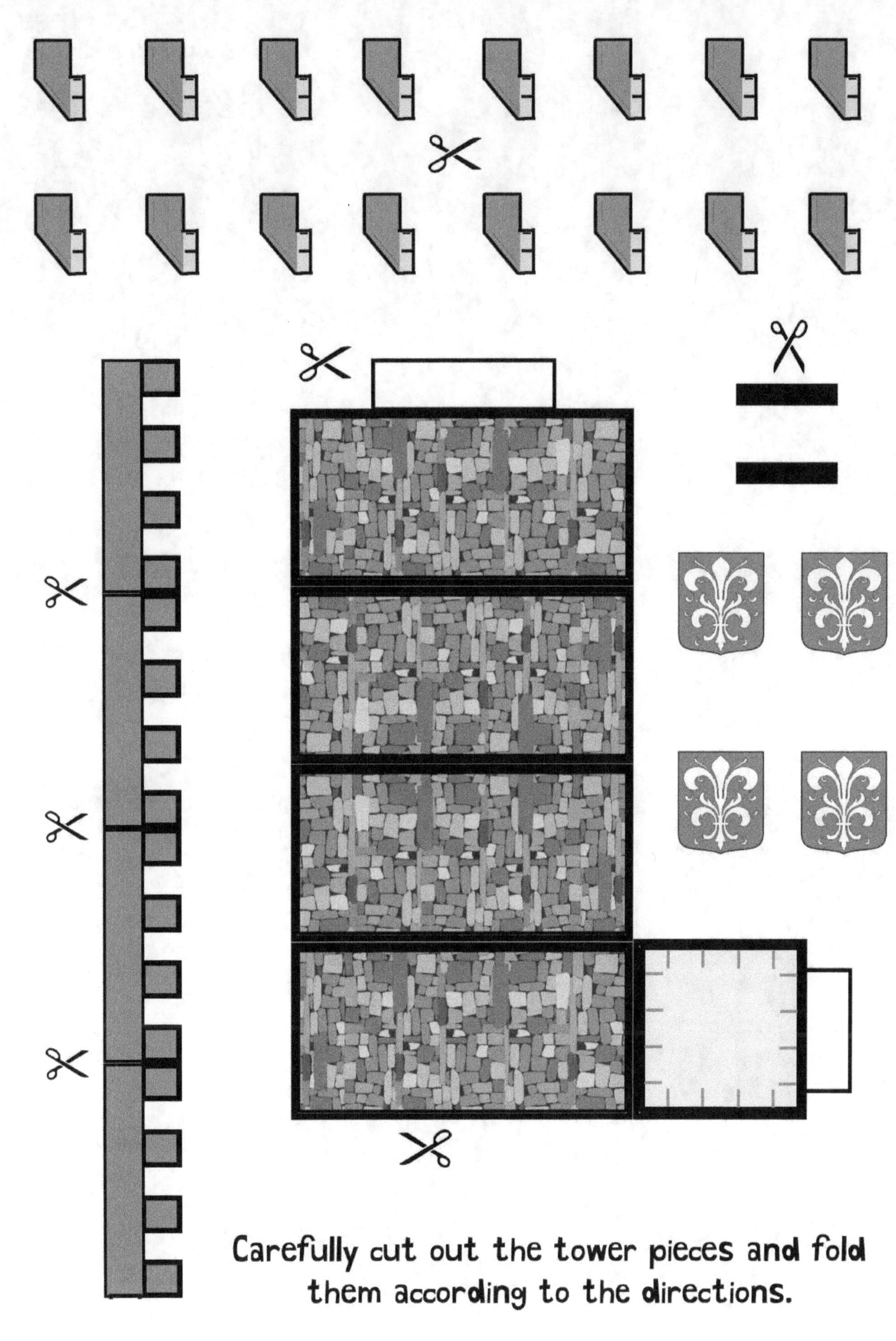

Carefully cut out the tower pieces and fold
them according to the directions.

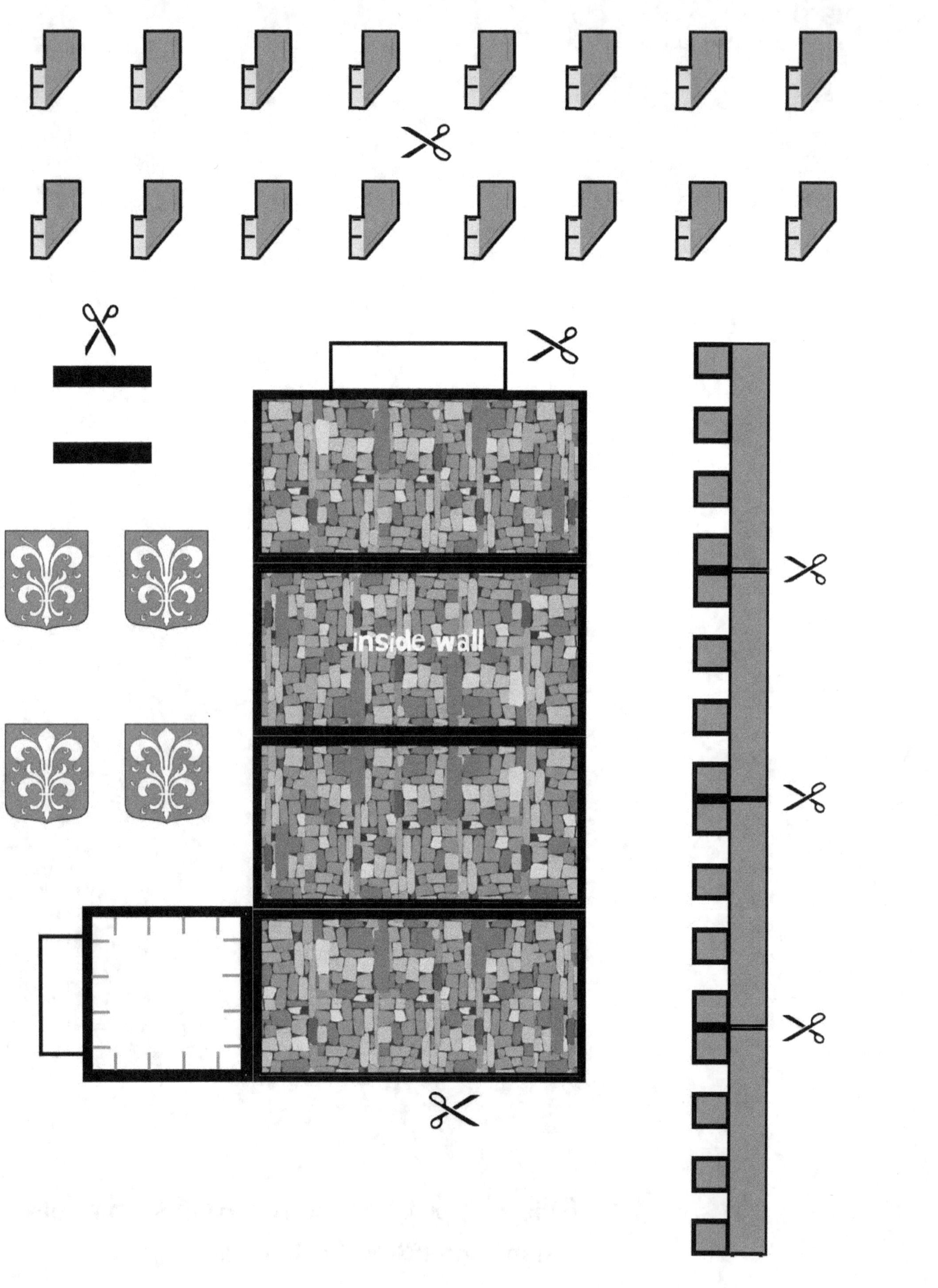

inside wall

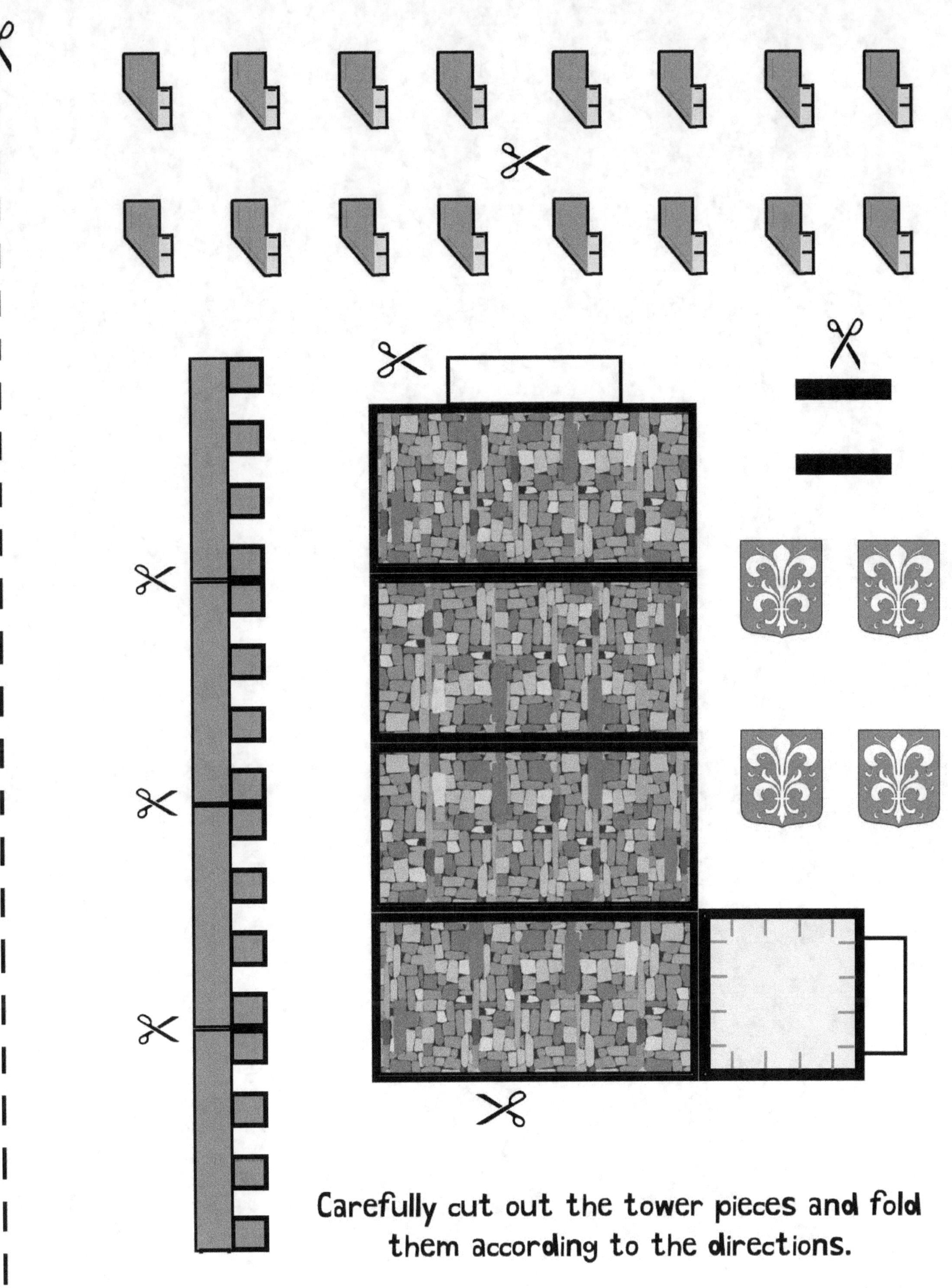

Carefully cut out the tower pieces and fold
them according to the directions.

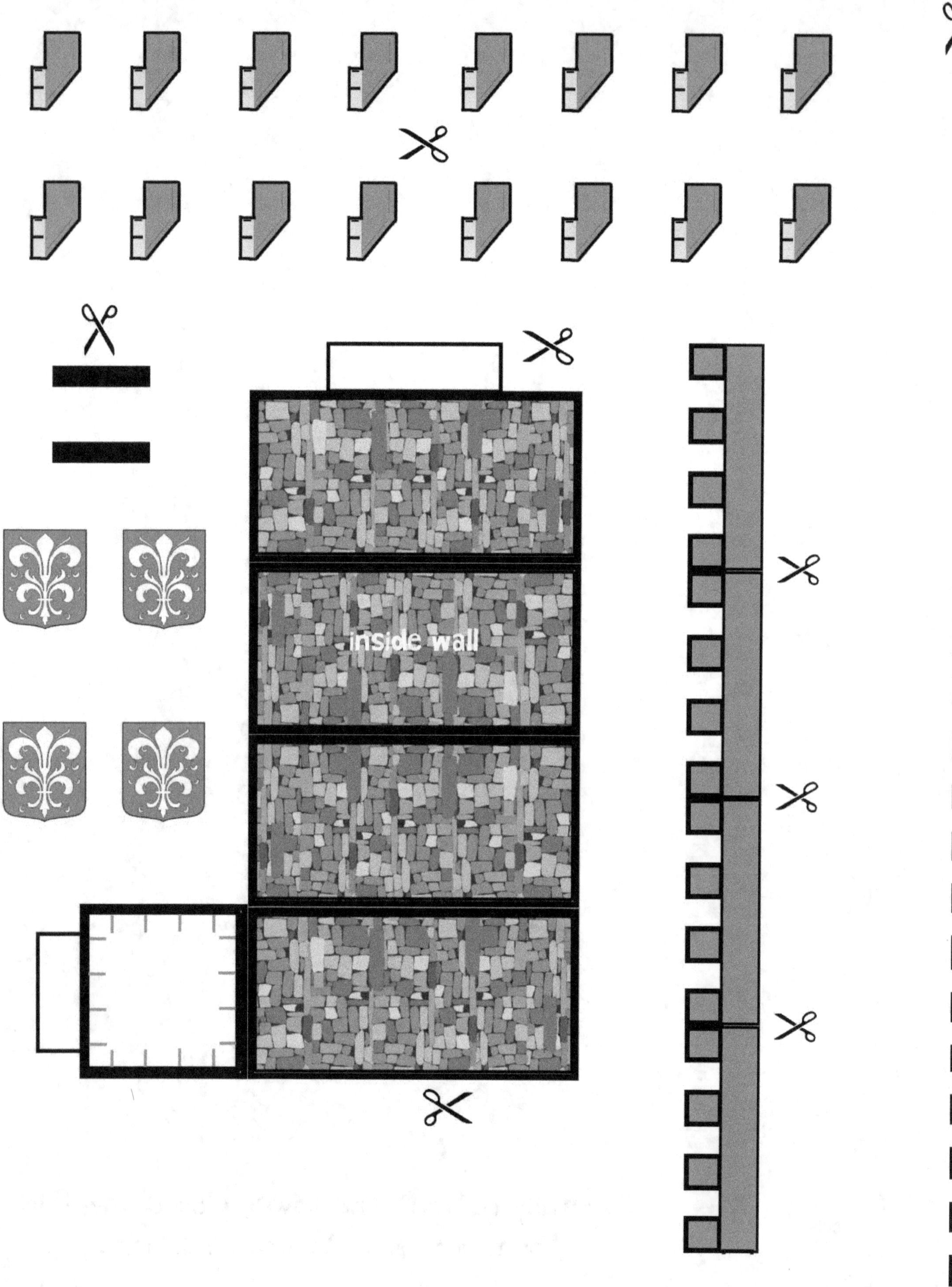
inside wall

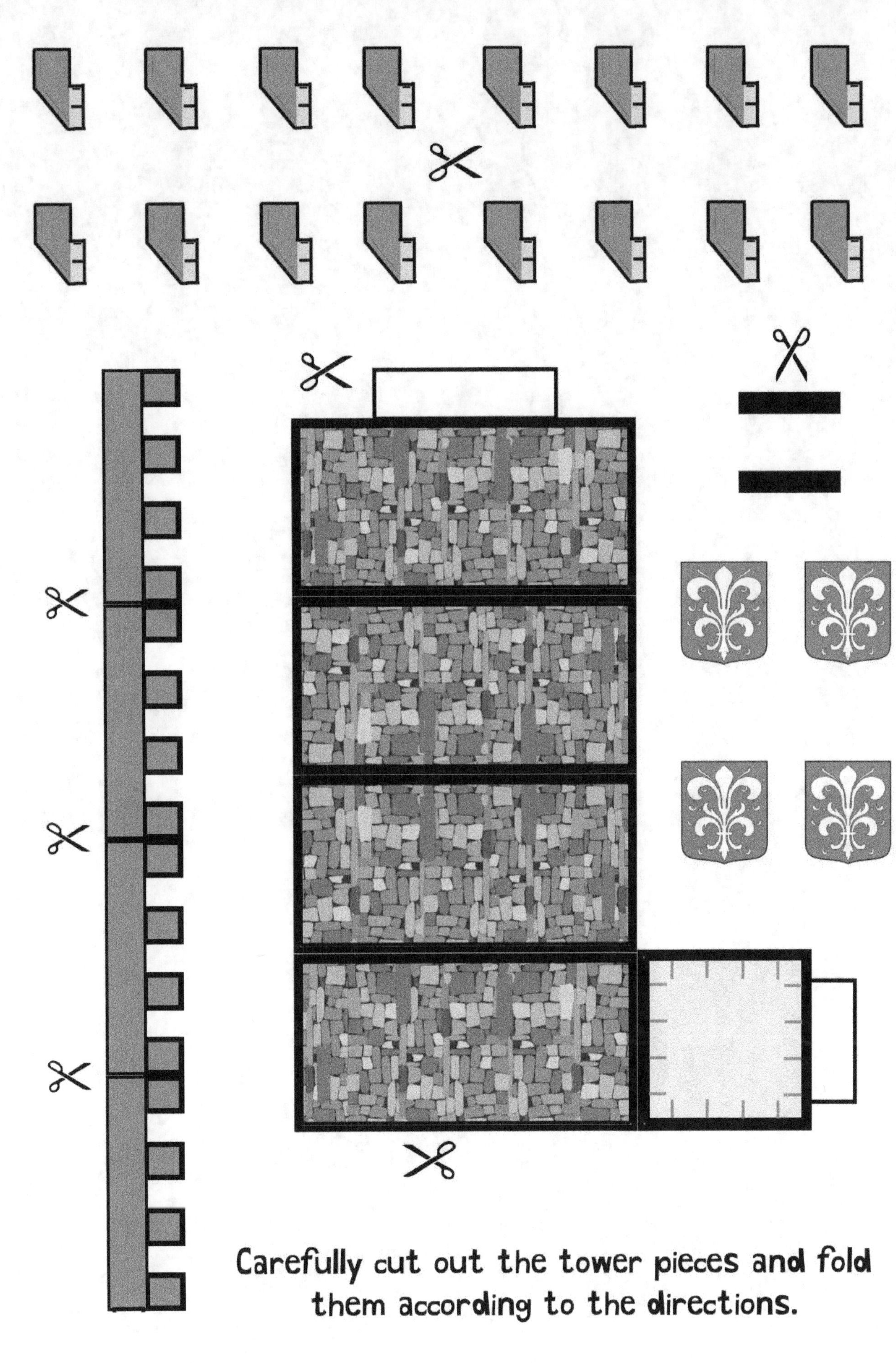

Carefully cut out the tower pieces and fold
them according to the directions.

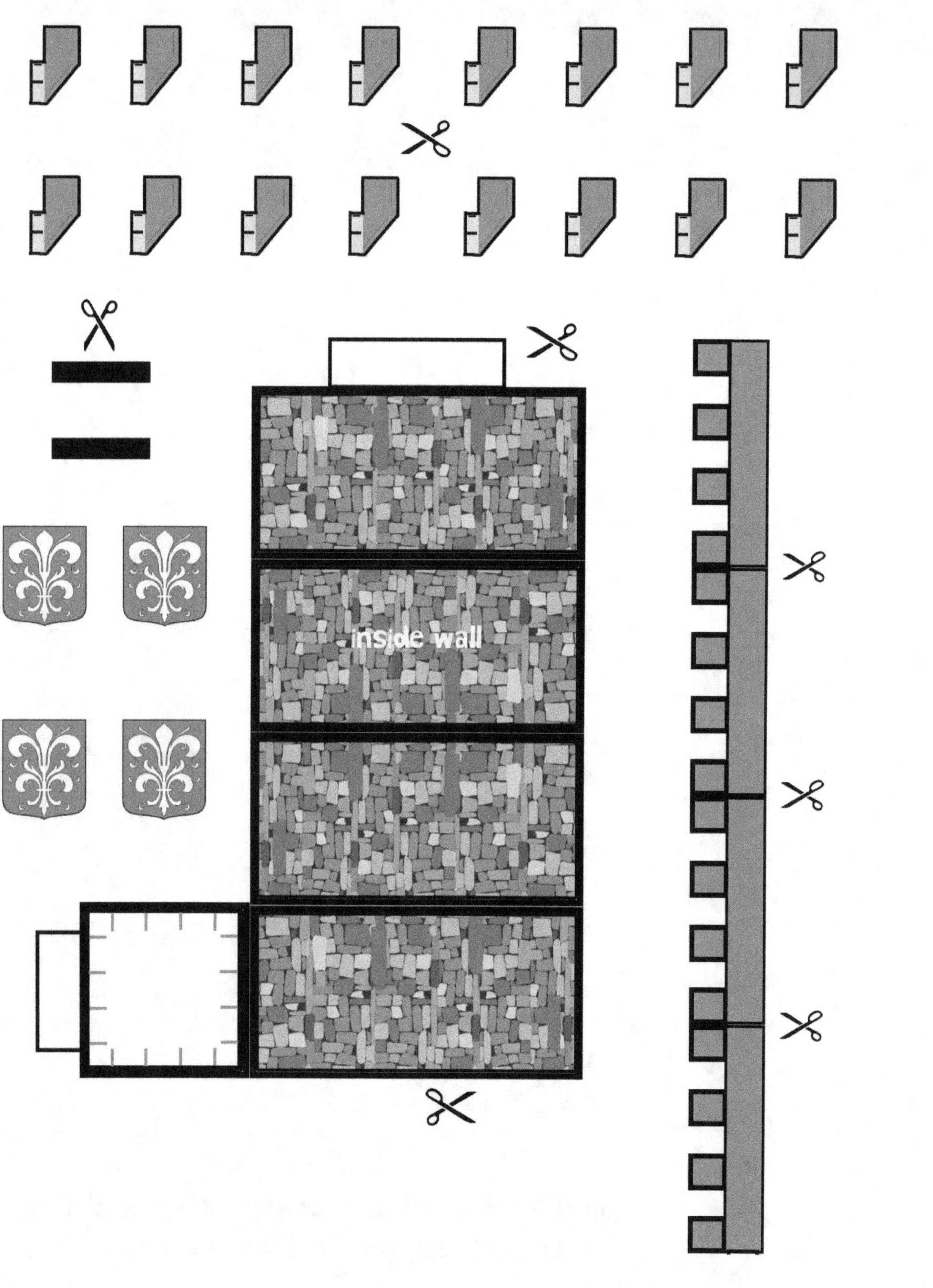

inside wall

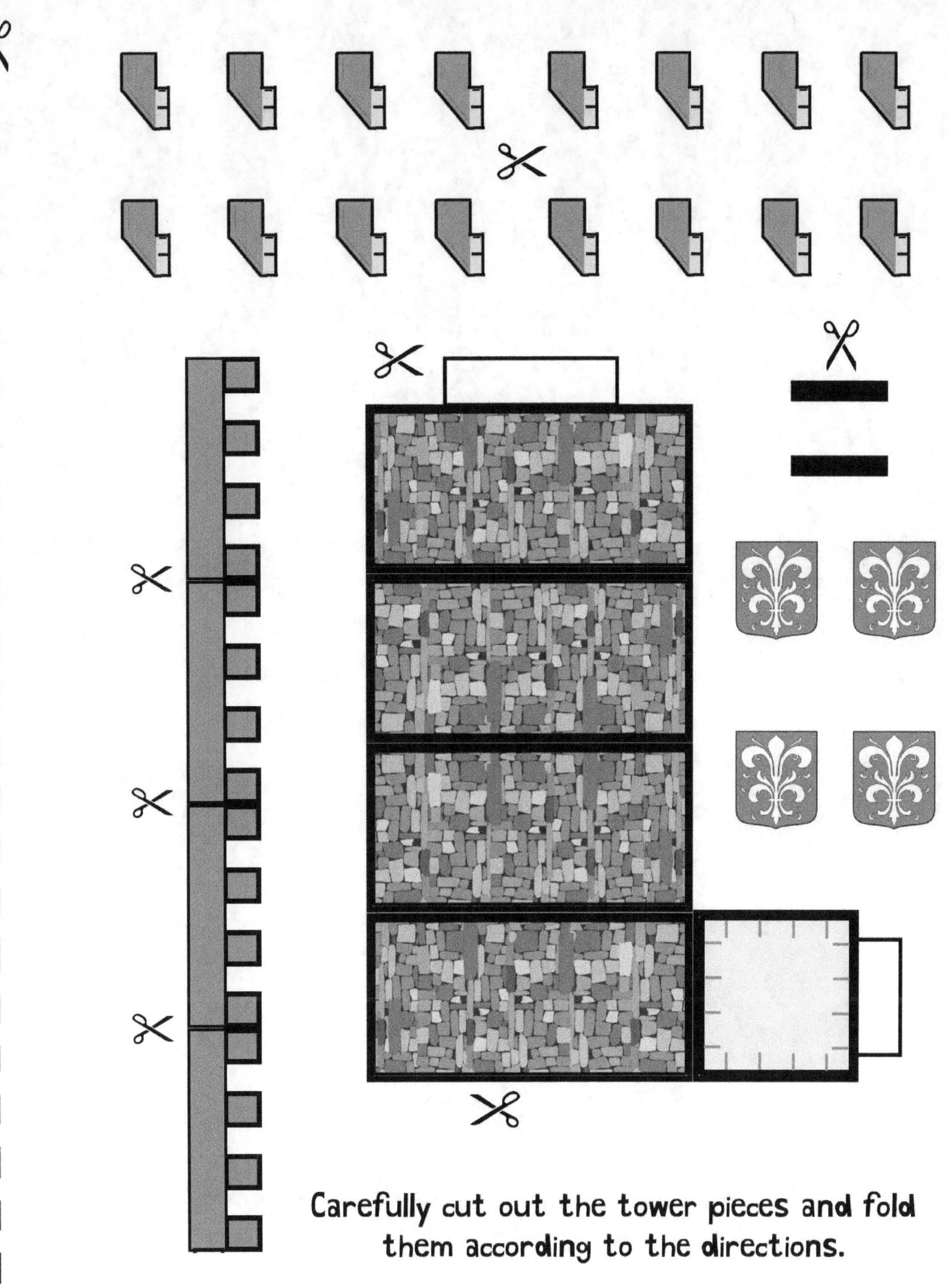

Carefully cut out the tower pieces and fold
them according to the directions.

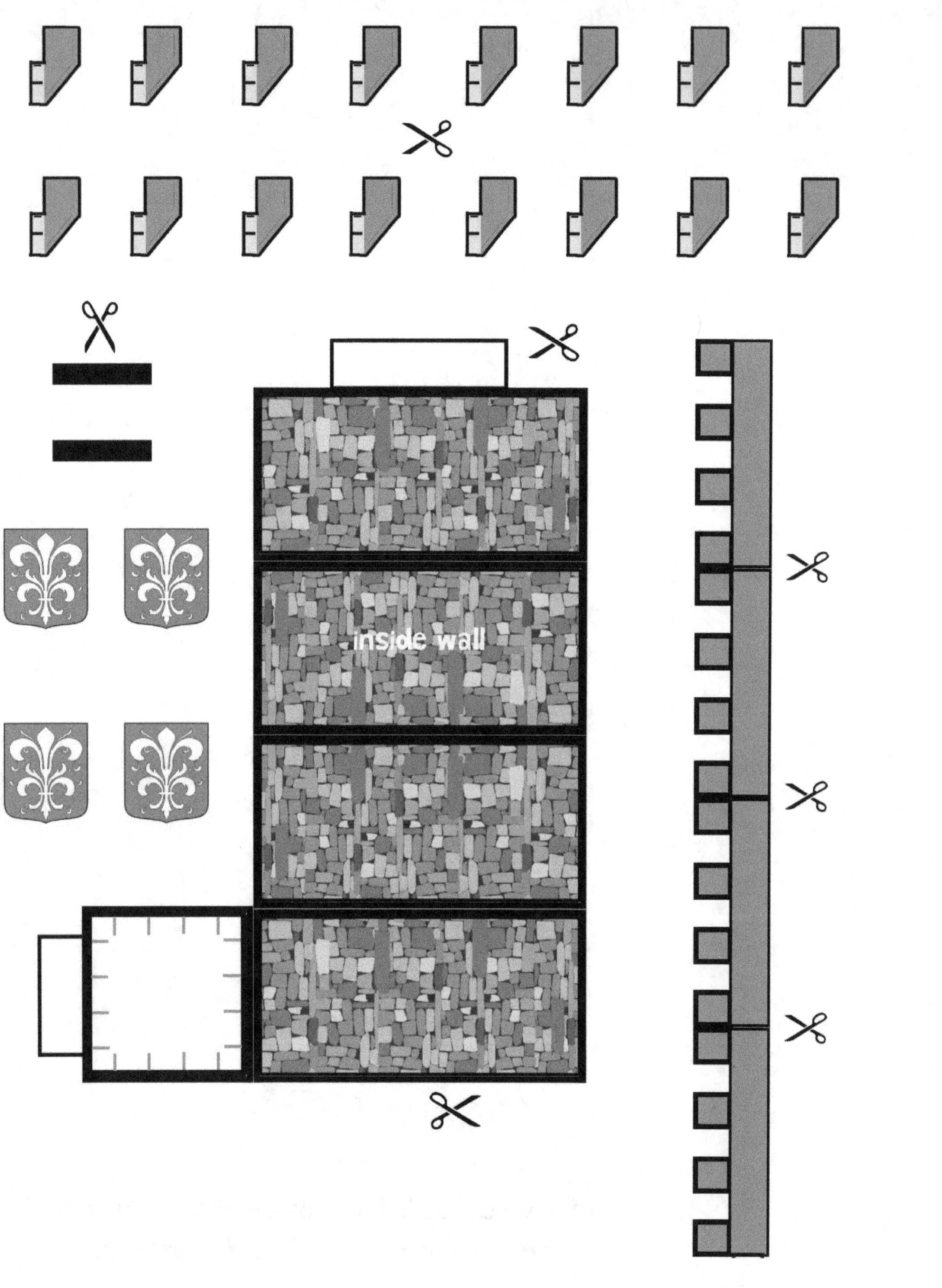

inside wall

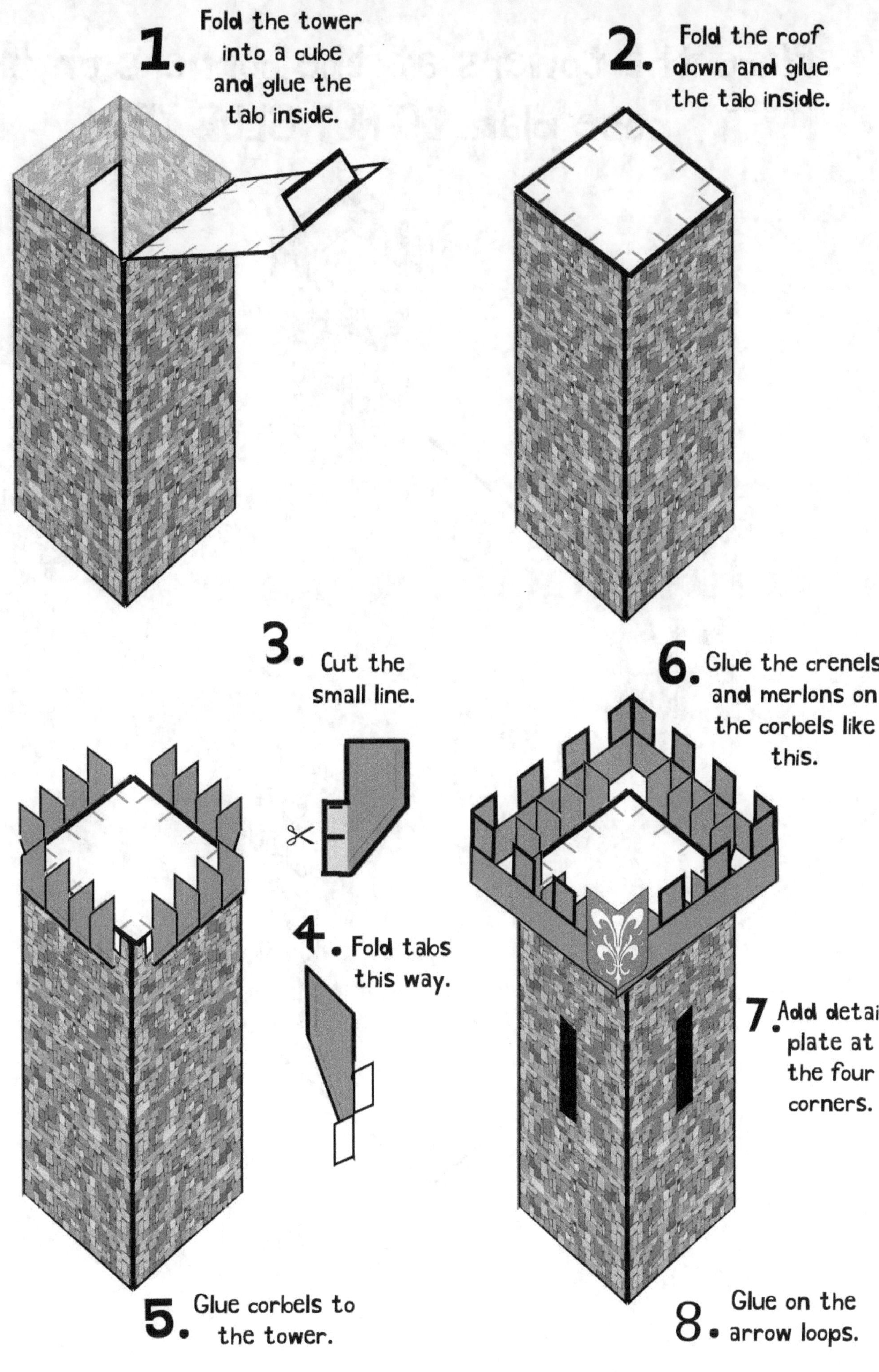

1. Fold the tower into a cube and glue the tab inside.
2. Fold the roof down and glue the tab inside.
3. Cut the small line.
4. Fold tabs this way.
5. Glue corbels to the tower.
6. Glue the crenels and merlons on the corbels like this.
7. Add detail plate at the four corners.
8. Glue on the arrow loops.

Place the towers at the corners on the base plan. DO NOT GLUE YET!

Medieval castle builders used some weird tools.
Can you find them in the puzzle?

MORTAR- A stone bowl used to mix cement.

PESTLE- A wood or stone club used to grind materials.

WINDLASS- A device to lift heavy objects like a drawbridge.

GOUGE- A tool for carving and shaping wood.

HOD- A box with a handle used to carry bricks & mortar.

ADZE- A tool used for shaping wood.

MAUL- A wooden sledgehammer.

WIMBLE- A hand-operated drill.

Help the stone mason get the stones from the quarry to the castle site.

CURTAIN WALLS

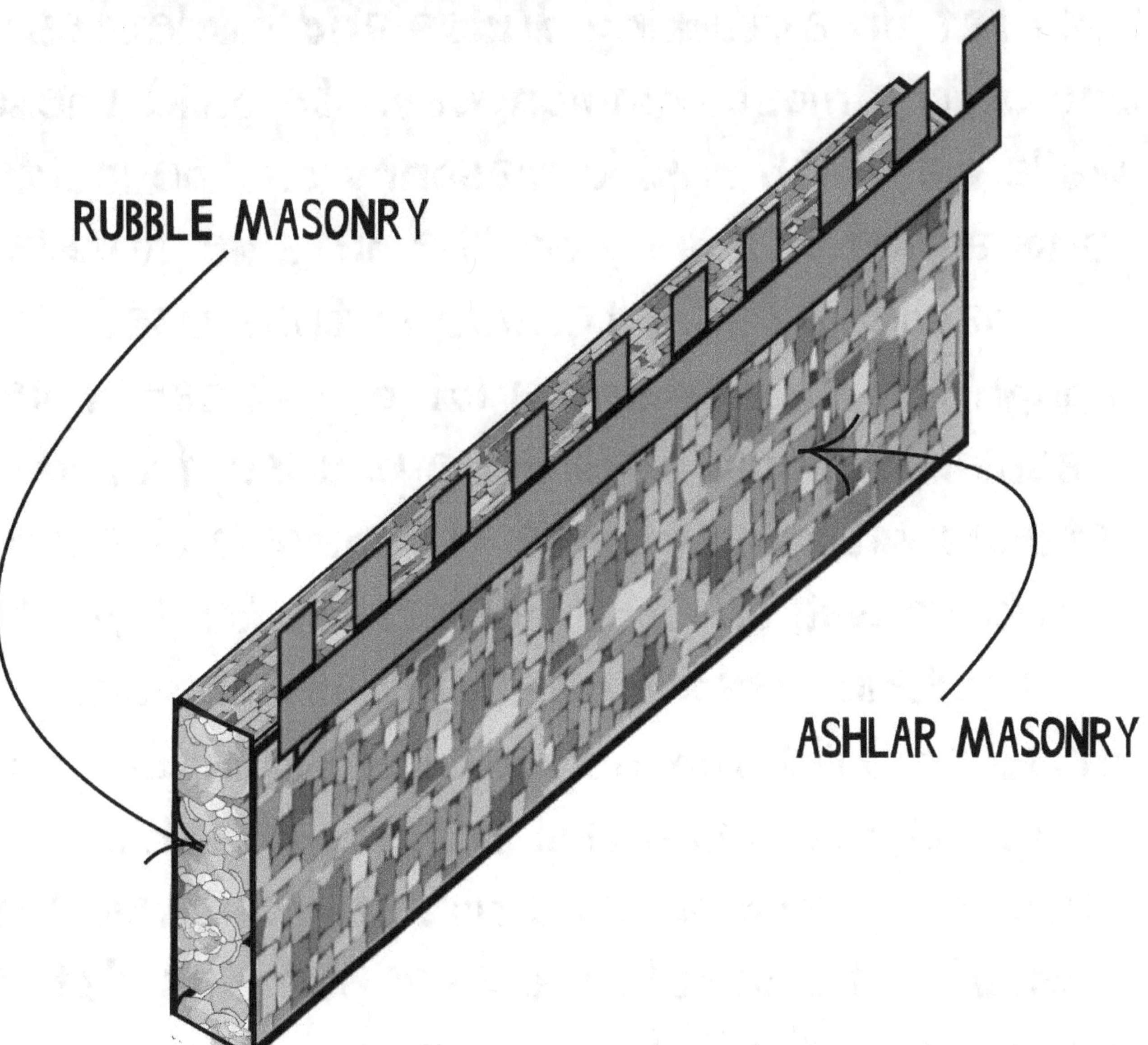

Think of a curtain wall as a big thick stone fence. These walls were built between the corner towers to keep the people who lived inside safe from invaders. They went around the perimeter of the bailey and had walkways on top with crenels, merlons, and machicolations where guards could shoot arrows and/or drop flaming rocks covered in pig fat on attacking dudes and dudettes. One of the most common ways to build these walls was with rubble masonry on the inside and ashlar masonry on the outside. Rubble masonry was a technique that used rough-cut stones and a lot of mortar while ashlar masonry was more precise, fitted stones with less mortar to make a cleaner pattern wall on the outside. The best part of rubble masonry was it was fast and cheap to build and made a strong inner core for the curtain wall. The use of ashlar masonry on the outside not only showed the wealth of the castle owner but was flat making it difficult for the enemy to climb up.

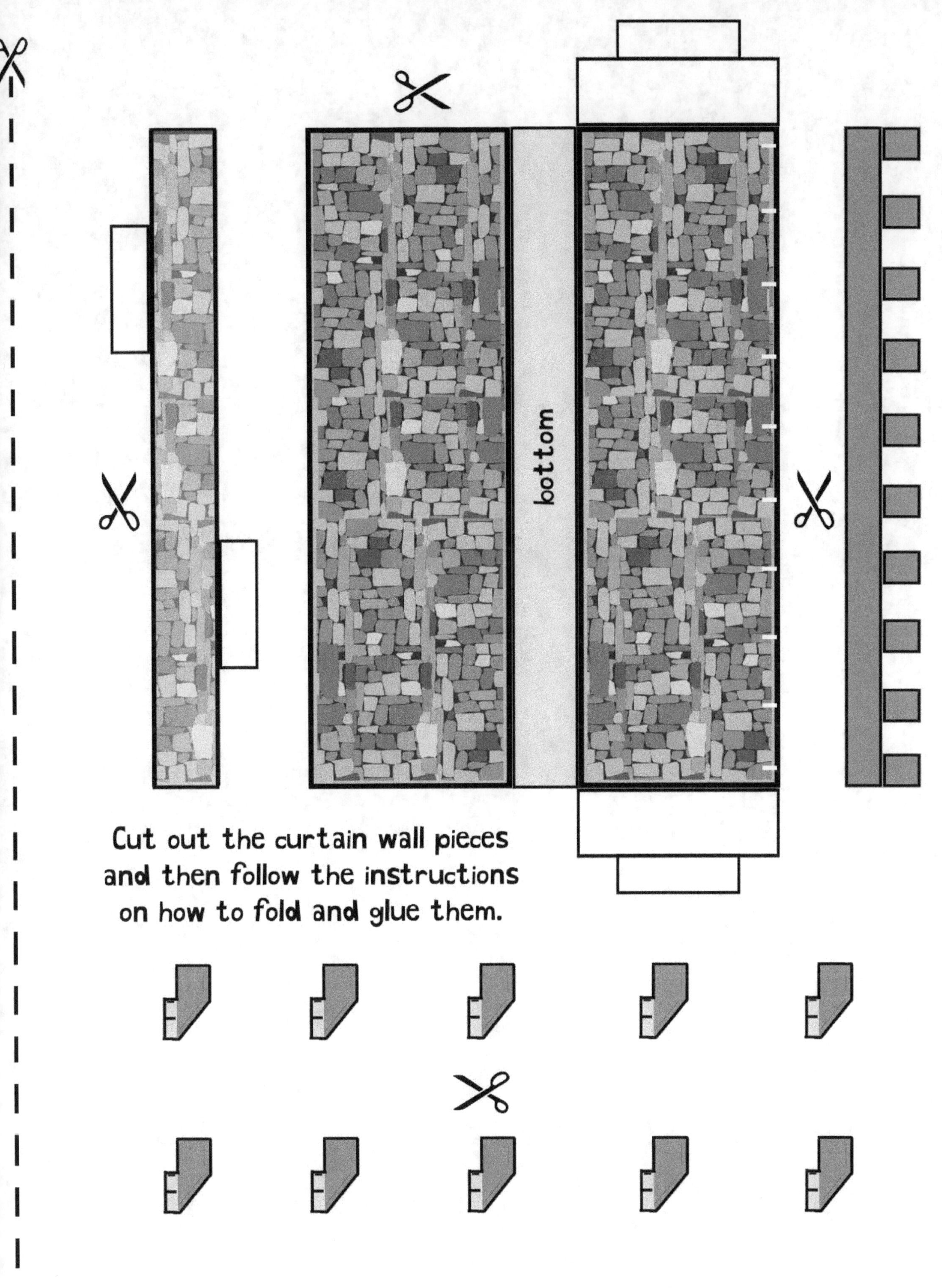
bottom
Cut out the curtain wall pieces
and then follow the instructions
on how to fold and glue them.

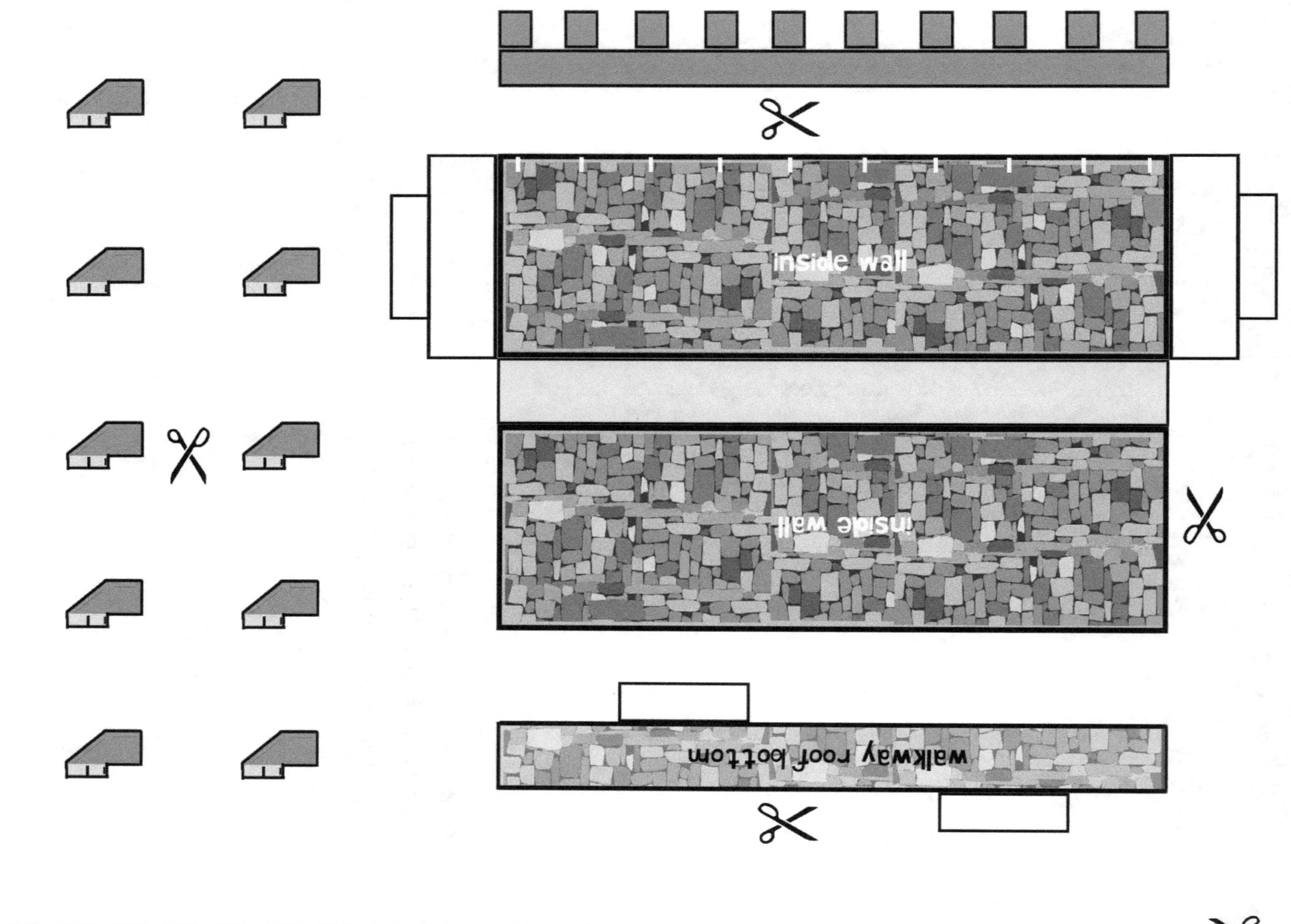

inside wall
inside wall
walkway roof bottom

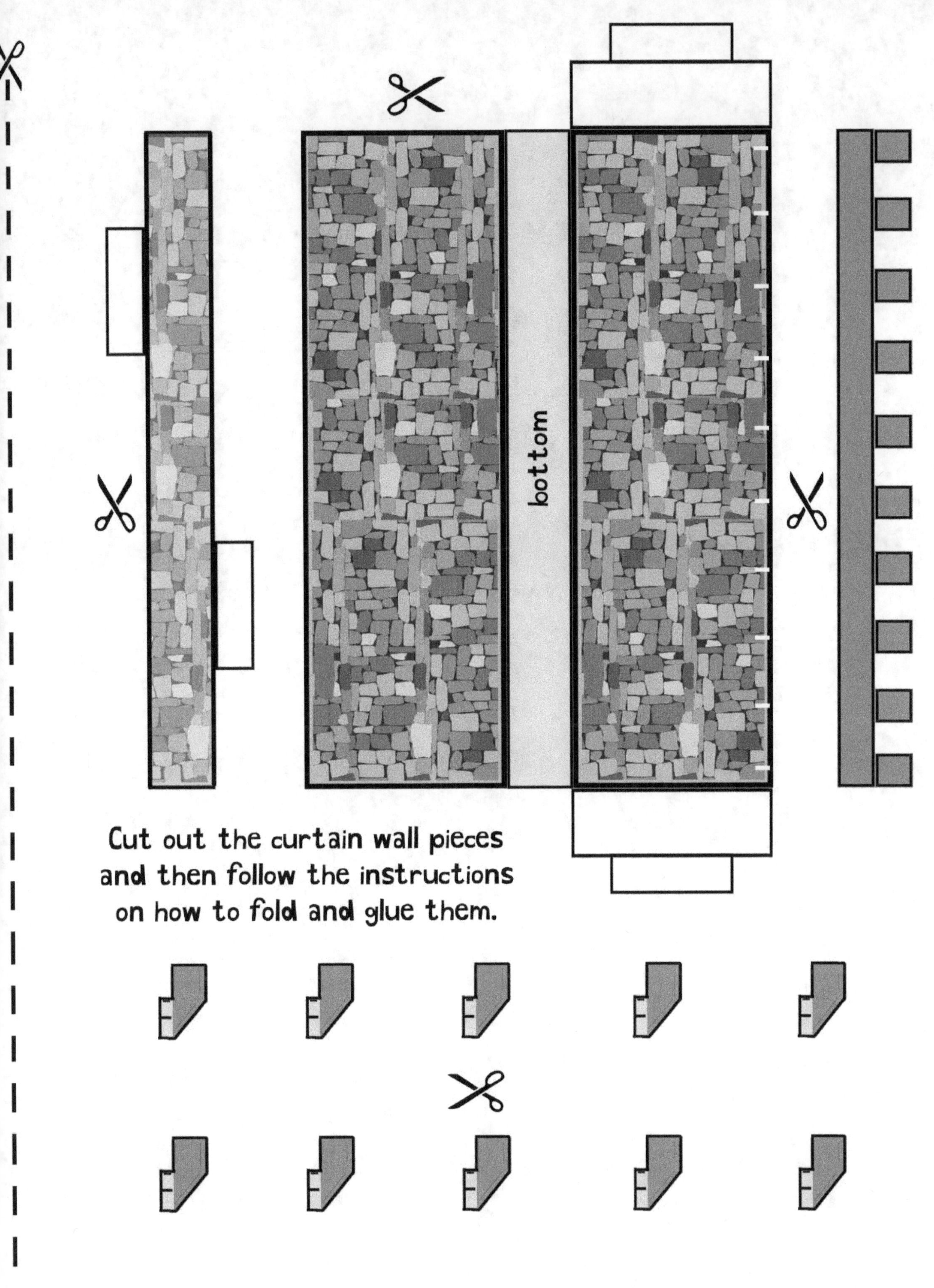

bottom
Cut out the curtain wall pieces
and then follow the instructions
on how to fold and glue them.

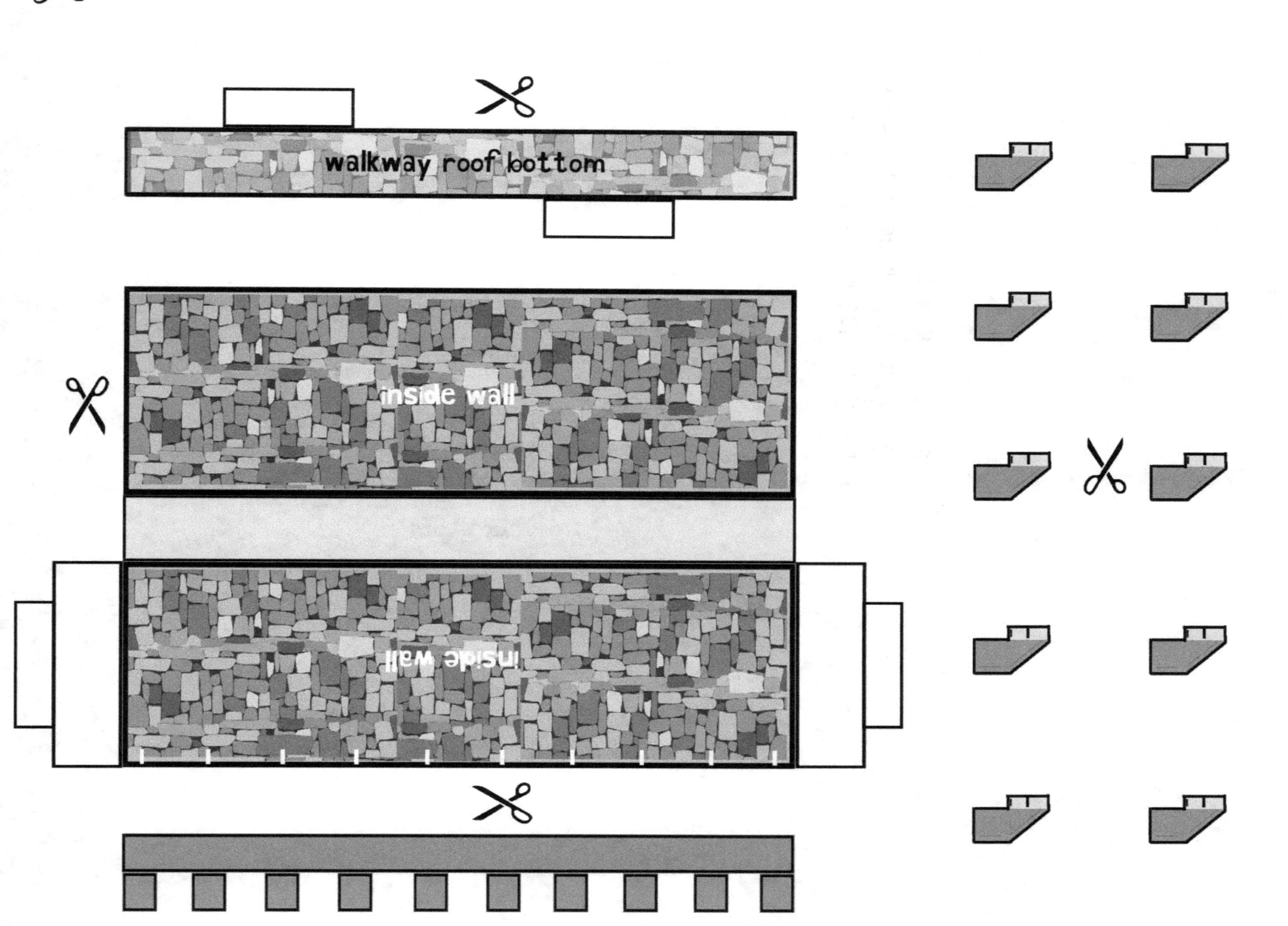

walkway roof bottom
inside wall
inside wall

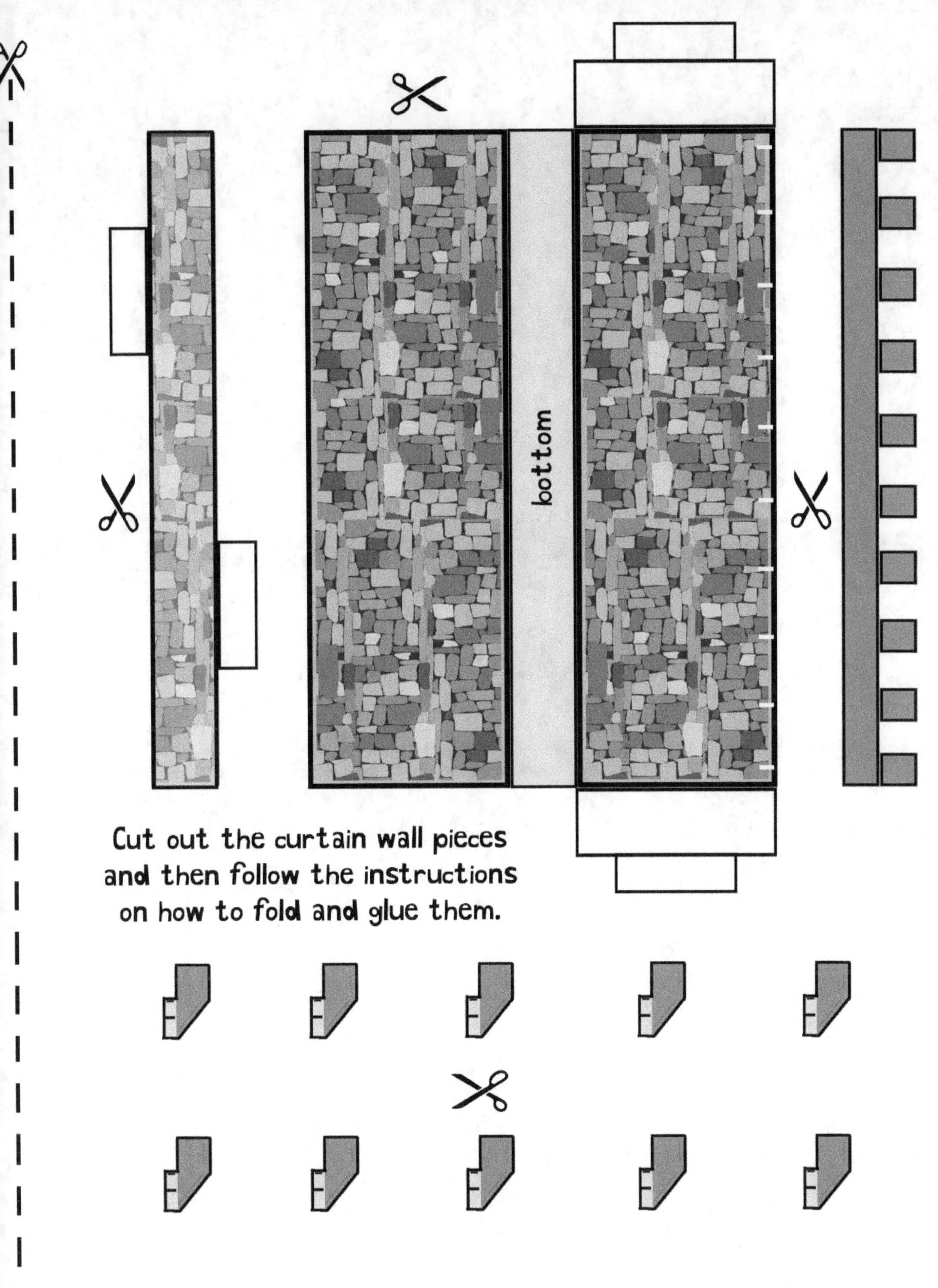

bottom
Cut out the curtain wall pieces
and then follow the instructions
on how to fold and glue them.

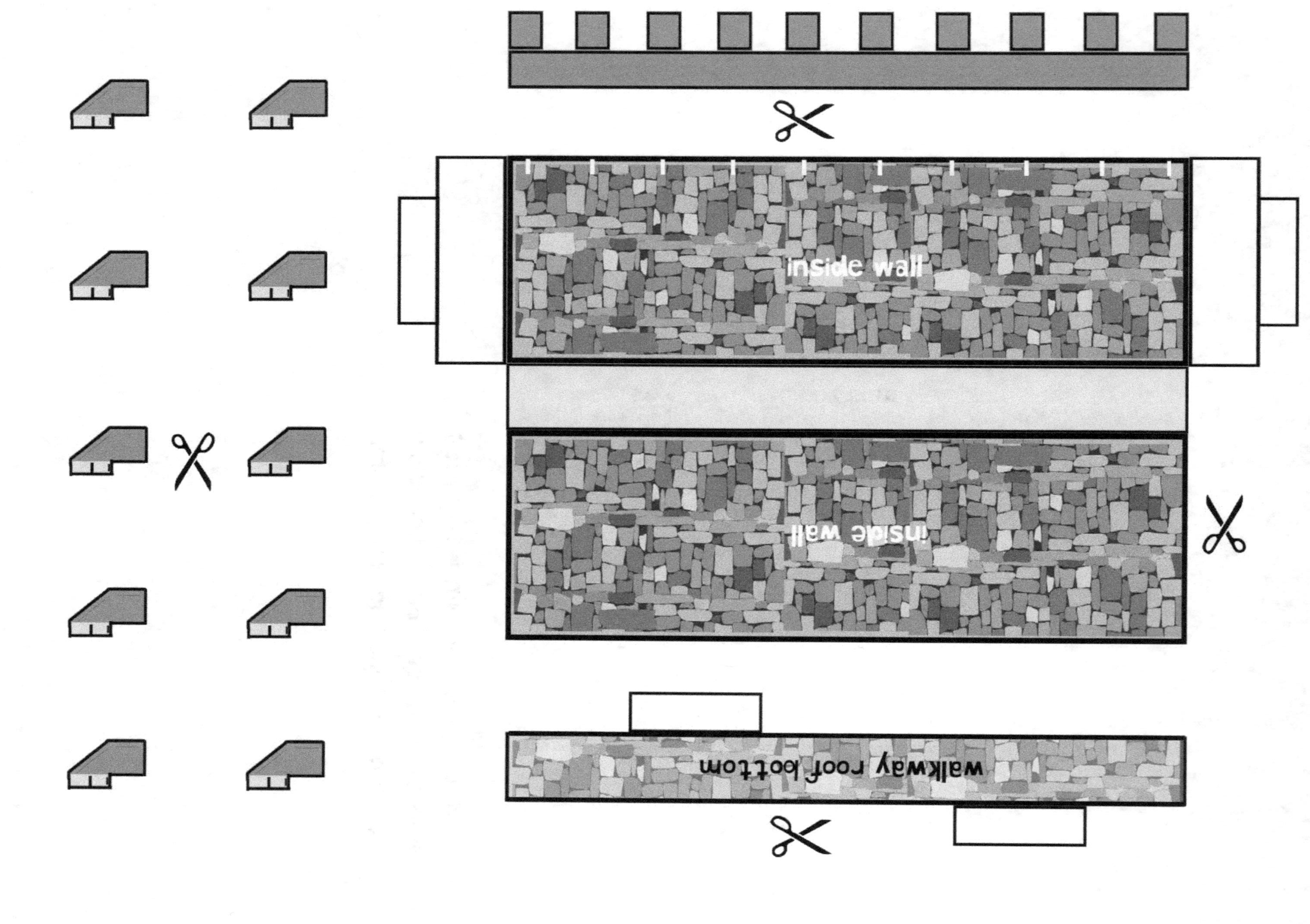

inside wall
inside wall
walkway roof bottom

FRONT CURTAIN WALL

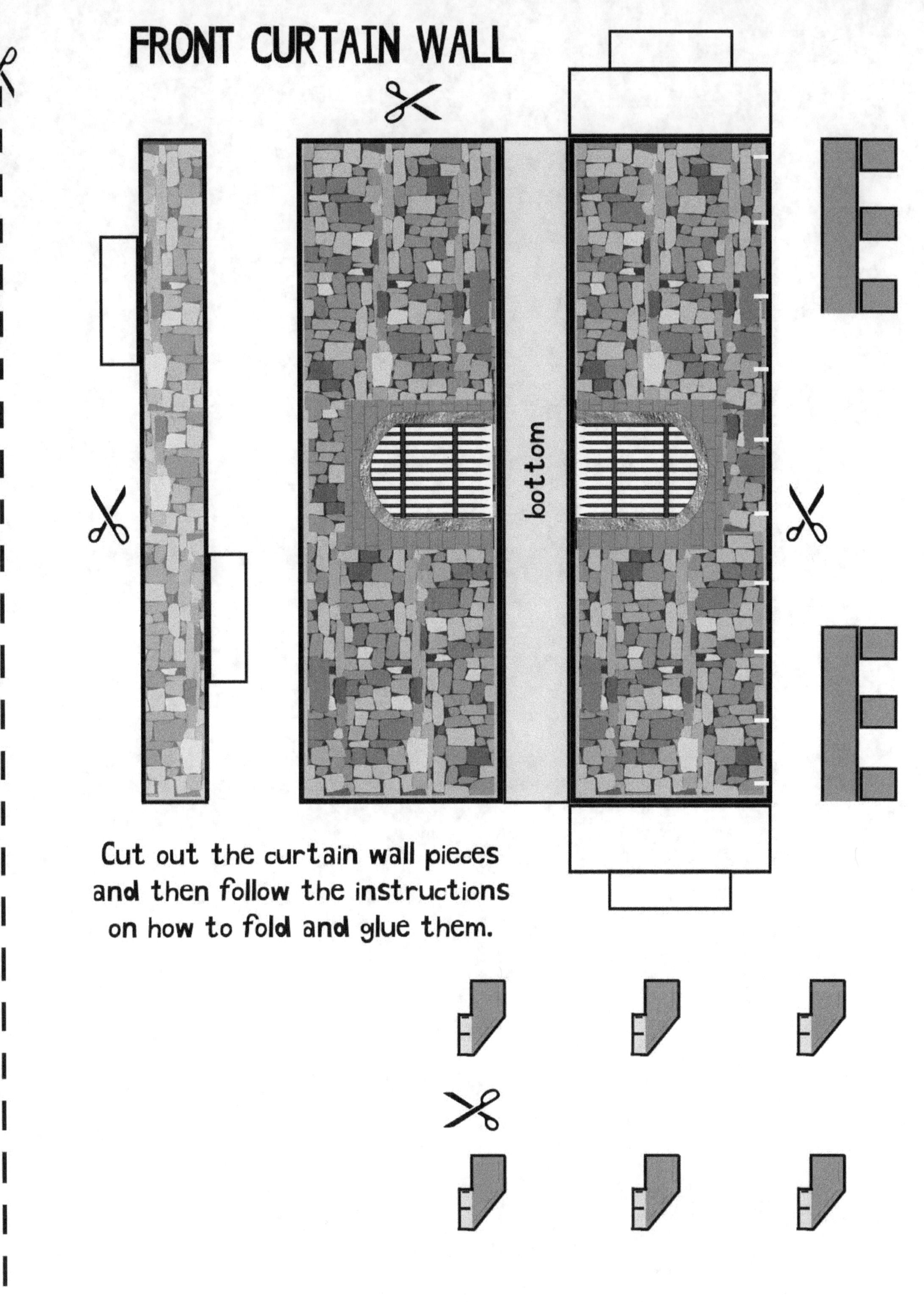

Cut out the curtain wall pieces
and then follow the instructions
on how to fold and glue them.

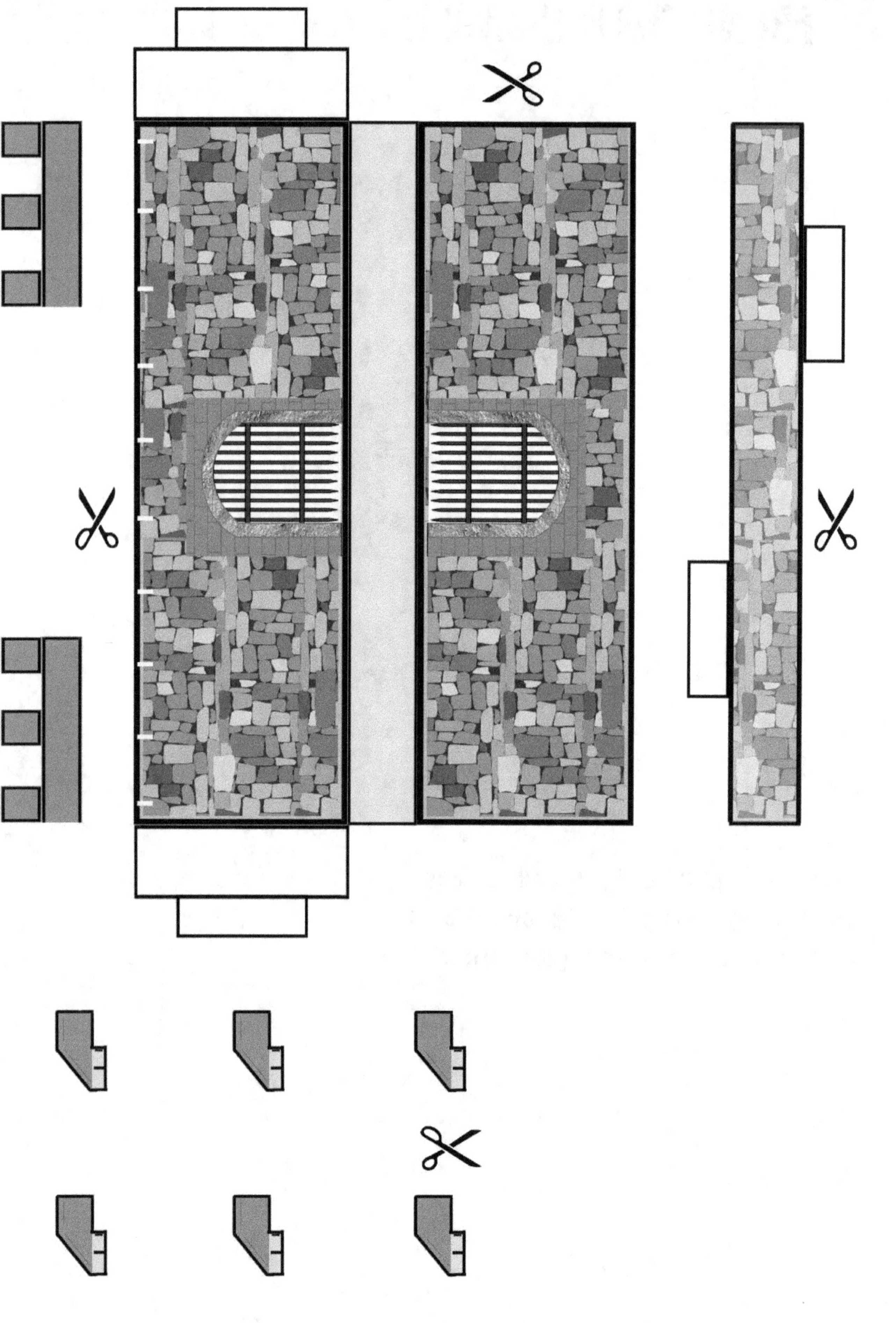

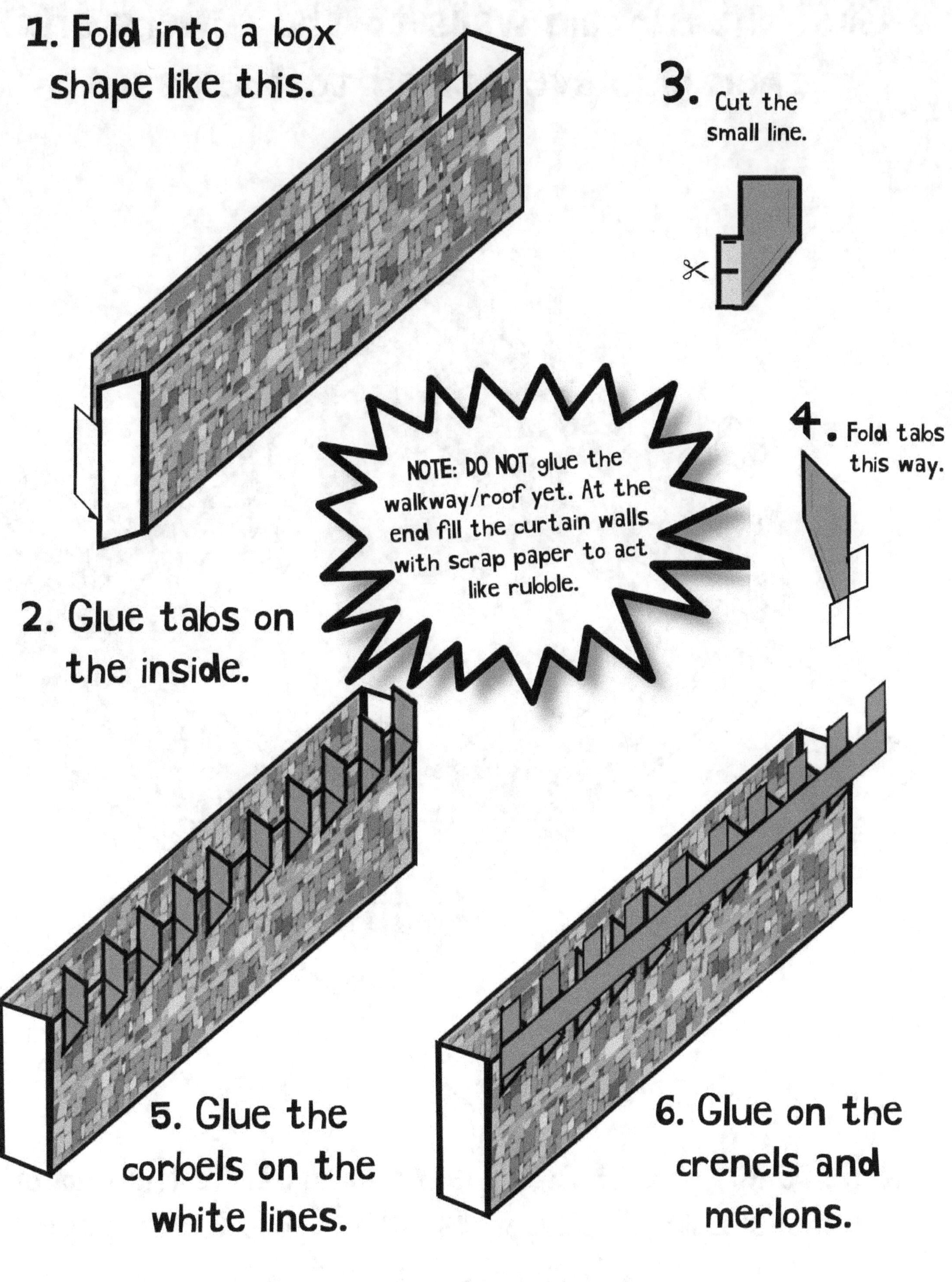

1. Fold into a box shape like this.

2. Glue tabs on the inside.

3. Cut the small line.

4. Fold tabs this way.

NOTE: DO NOT glue the walkway/roof yet. At the end fill the curtain walls with scrap paper to act like rubble.

5. Glue the corbels on the white lines.

6. Glue on the crenels and merlons.

Glue the curtain walls to the towers and then glue everything to the base.

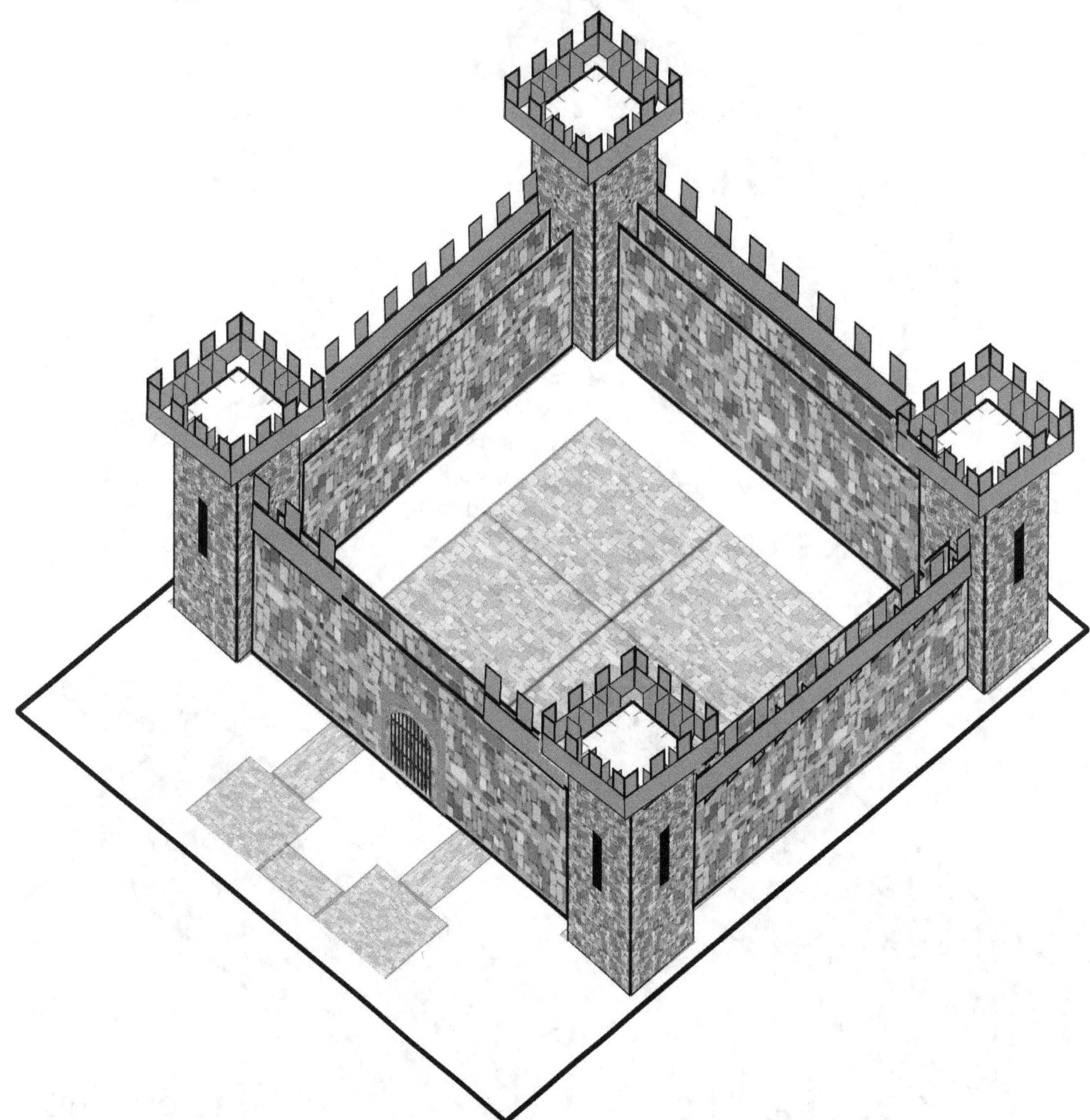

NOTE: DO NOT glue the walkway/roofs yet. At the end of the model build, fill the walls with rubble (scrap paper) and then glue the roofs on.

CASTLE PARTS

TURRET- Small structures on walls used for watching or shooting.

DONJON- Another word for the KEEP.

ARROW LOOPS- Little slits in the wall that let archers shoot arrows whilst being protected.

PORTCULLIS- A heavy gate that would block the entrance in a gatehouse.

DRAWBRIDGE- A gate that can be raised or lowered over a moat to control access into the castle.

MOAT- A trench filled with water surrounding the castle walls.

GARDEROBE- A castle bathroom.

DUNGEON- Dark underground rooms used to hold prisoners and/or food supplies.

SOLAR- A private room on an upper floor reserved for the castle's owner and their family.

OUBLIETTE- A prison cell with one door and no windows.

CASTLE PARTS

ACROSS

2. Protects the gatehouse.
4. The castle's main tower.
6. A castle bathroom.
8. An iron gate.
9. A jail cell with no windows.

DOWN

1. Another name for a keep.
3. Open notch at the top of a castle.
5. A hole to drop flaming rocks through.
7. The opposite of a crenel.

GATEHOUSE

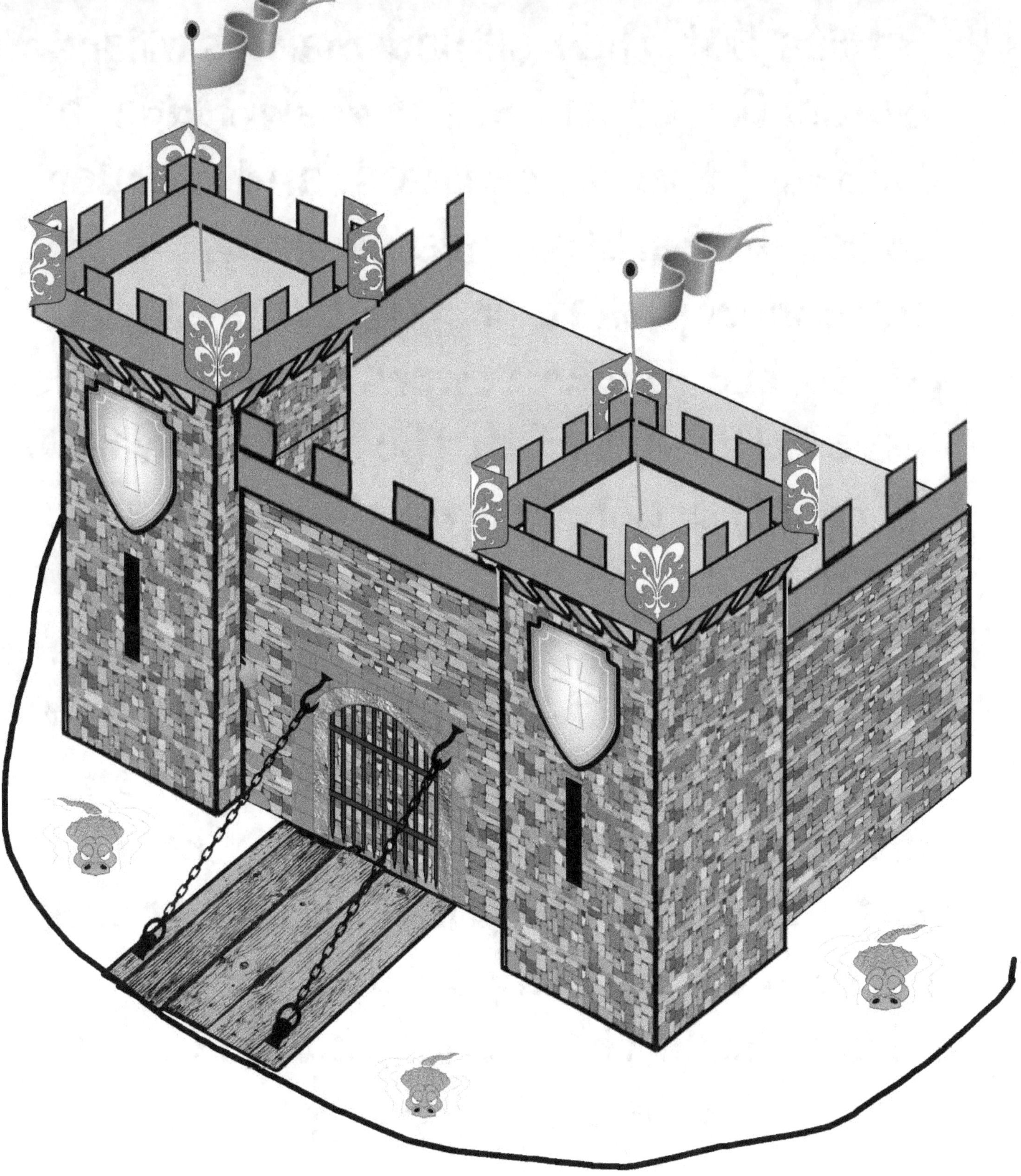

The gatehouse is basically the front door to the castle. There were different styles but they all had many similar pieces. Our castle has a drawbridge, a barbican, two portcullises, and murder holes. The barbican has two towers at the corners that are built in a similar way to the corner towers and the walls are built similar to the curtain wall construction. Drawbridges had a mechanism like a winch that could be cranked to raise and lower the bridge. The portcullis was usually lifted up and down with counterweights. When an enemy was caught in between the two portcullises the defenders could attack them by shooting arrows through murder holes that were installed in the walls and/or ceilings

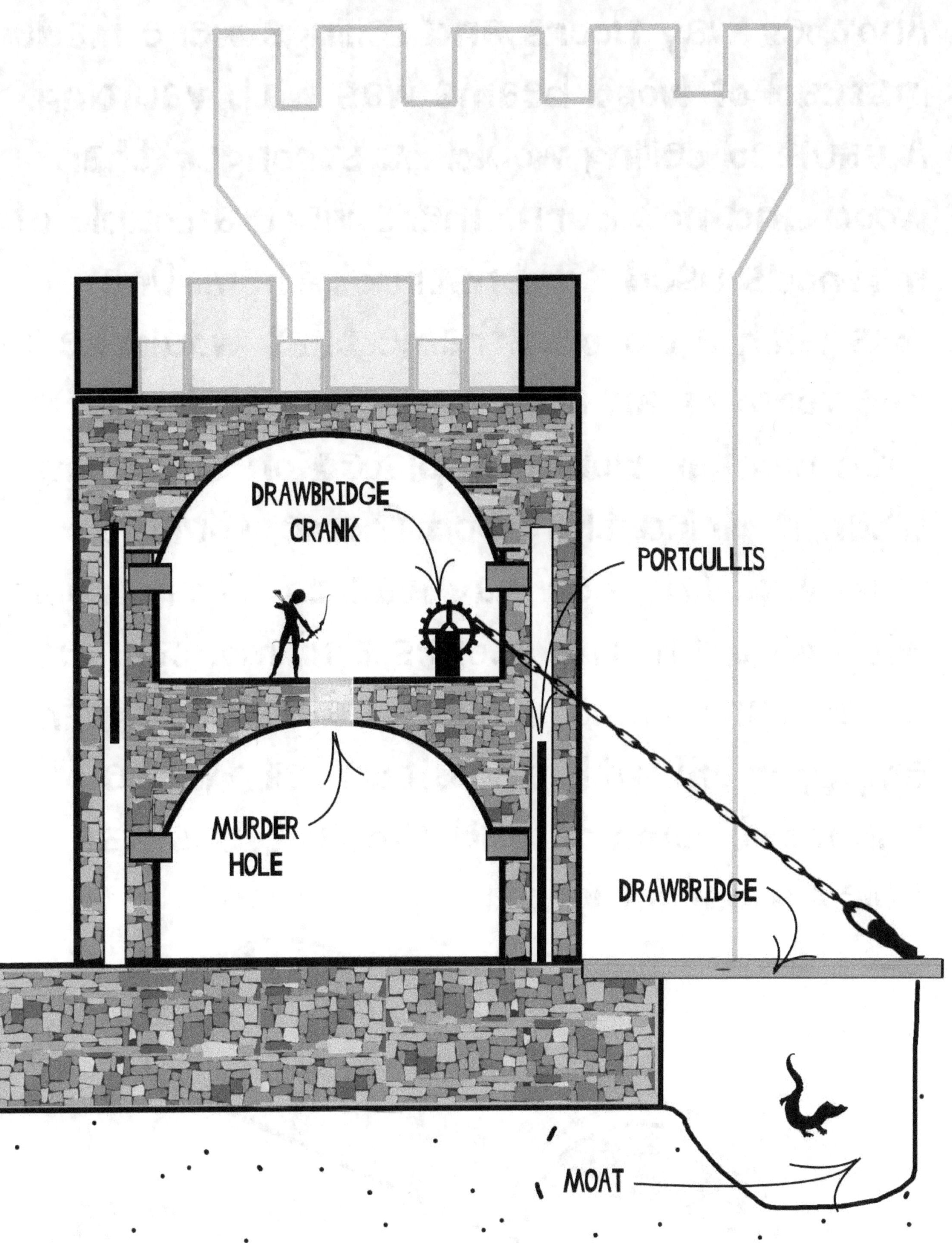

DRAWBRIDGE CRANK
PORTCULLIS
MURDER HOLE
DRAWBRIDGE
MOAT

Another way floors and ceilings were made instead of wood beams was with vaulting. A vaulted ceiling would be stronger than wood and not burn. There were a couple of methods used to construct them. One was with a wooden frame that would be in the form of an arch and stones stuck with mortar would be placed on the form. When it dried the wood frame would be removed. Another way was to fill the room with dirt, lay the stones and mortar, let it dry, and remove all the dirt leaving an empty room with a vaulted ceiling. One of the most common and simple types was called a barrel vault.

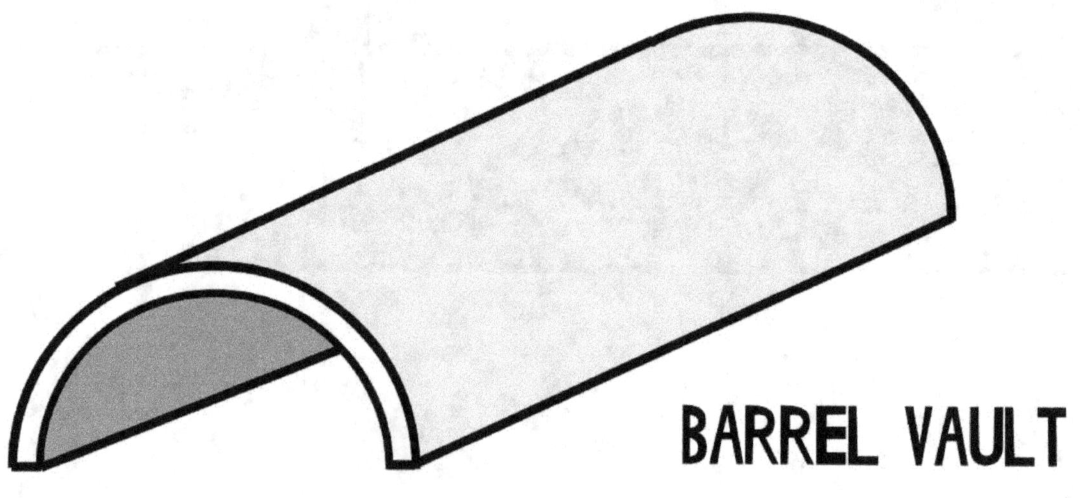

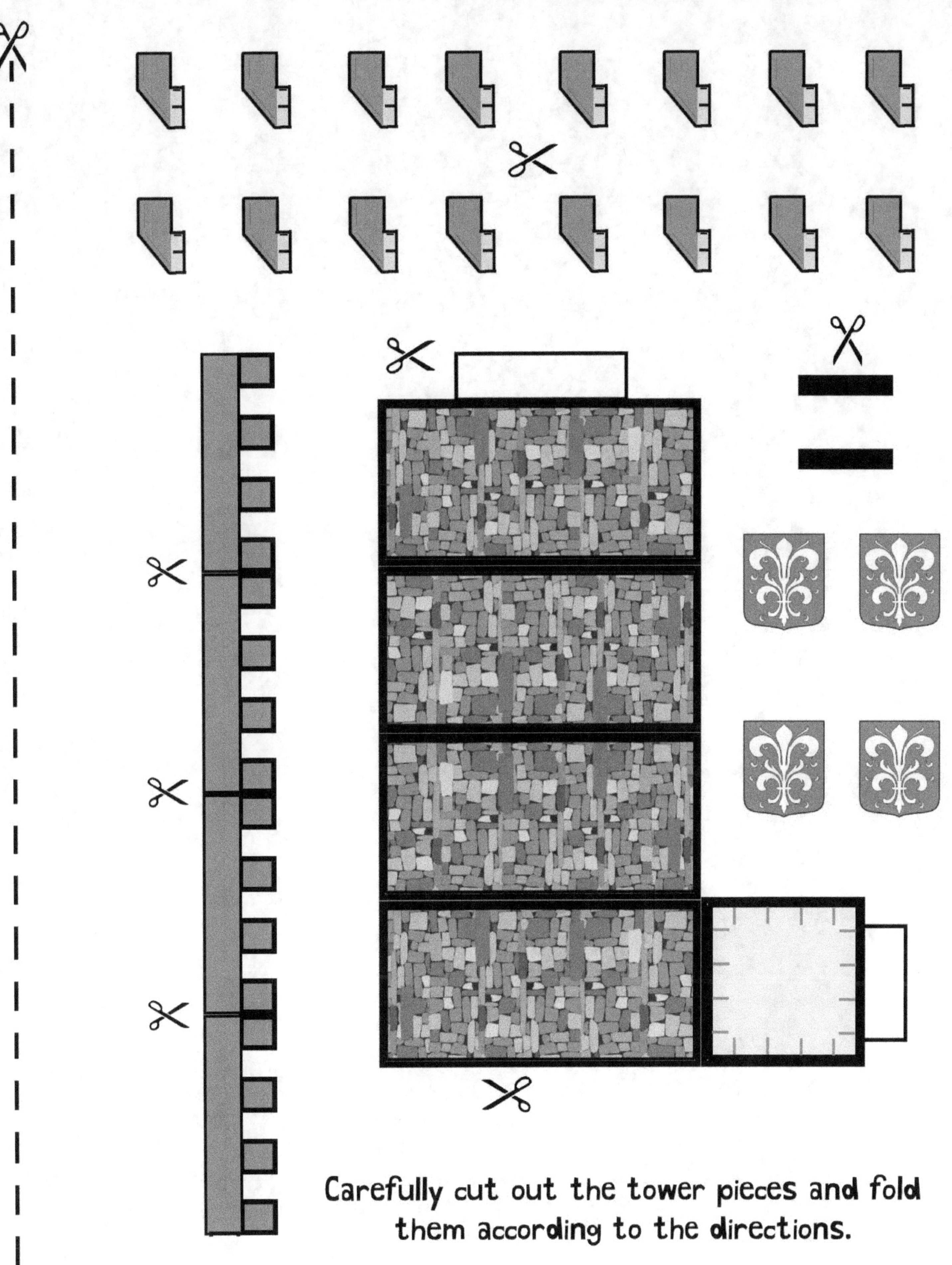

Carefully cut out the tower pieces and fold
them according to the directions.

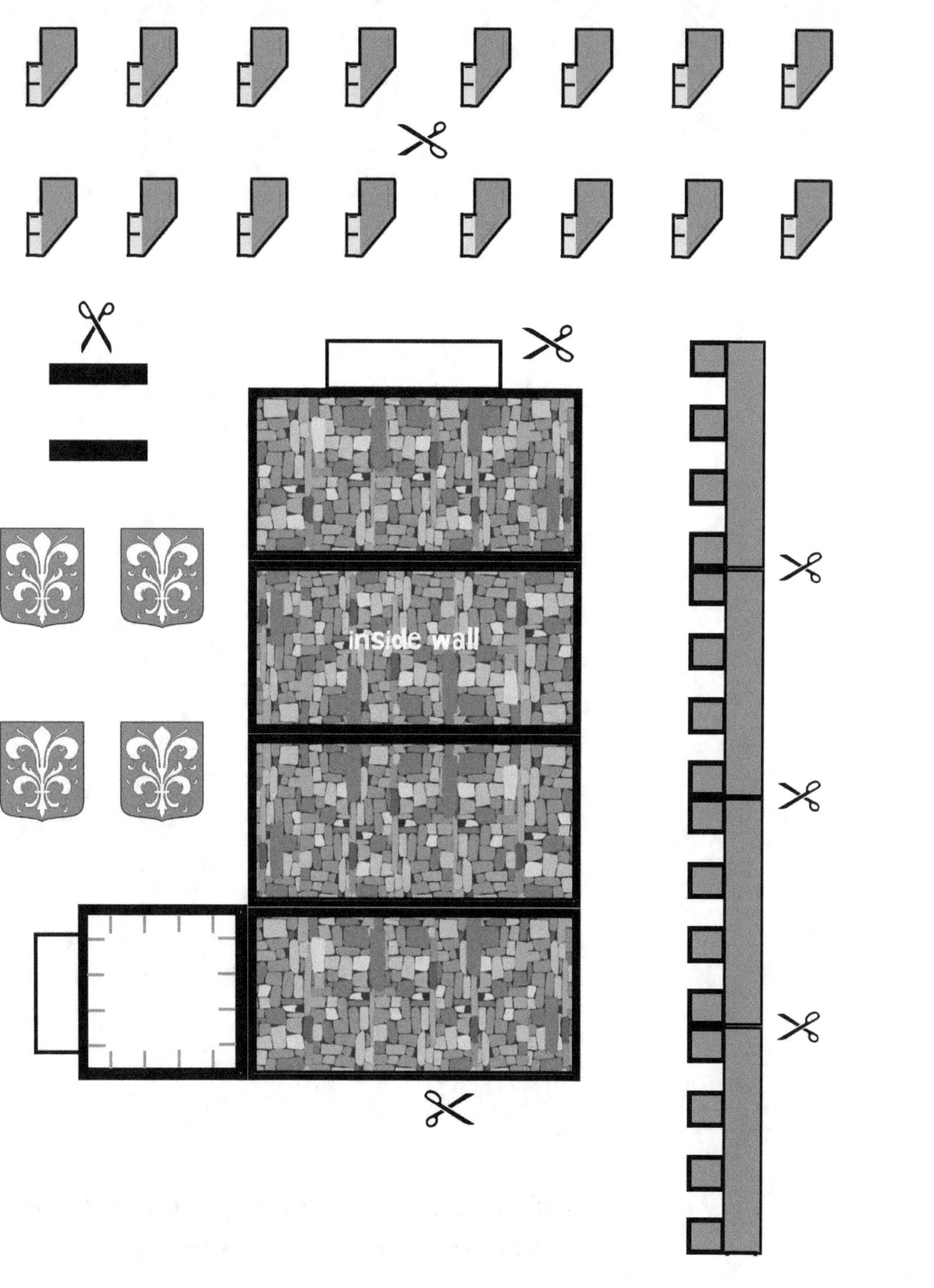

inside wall

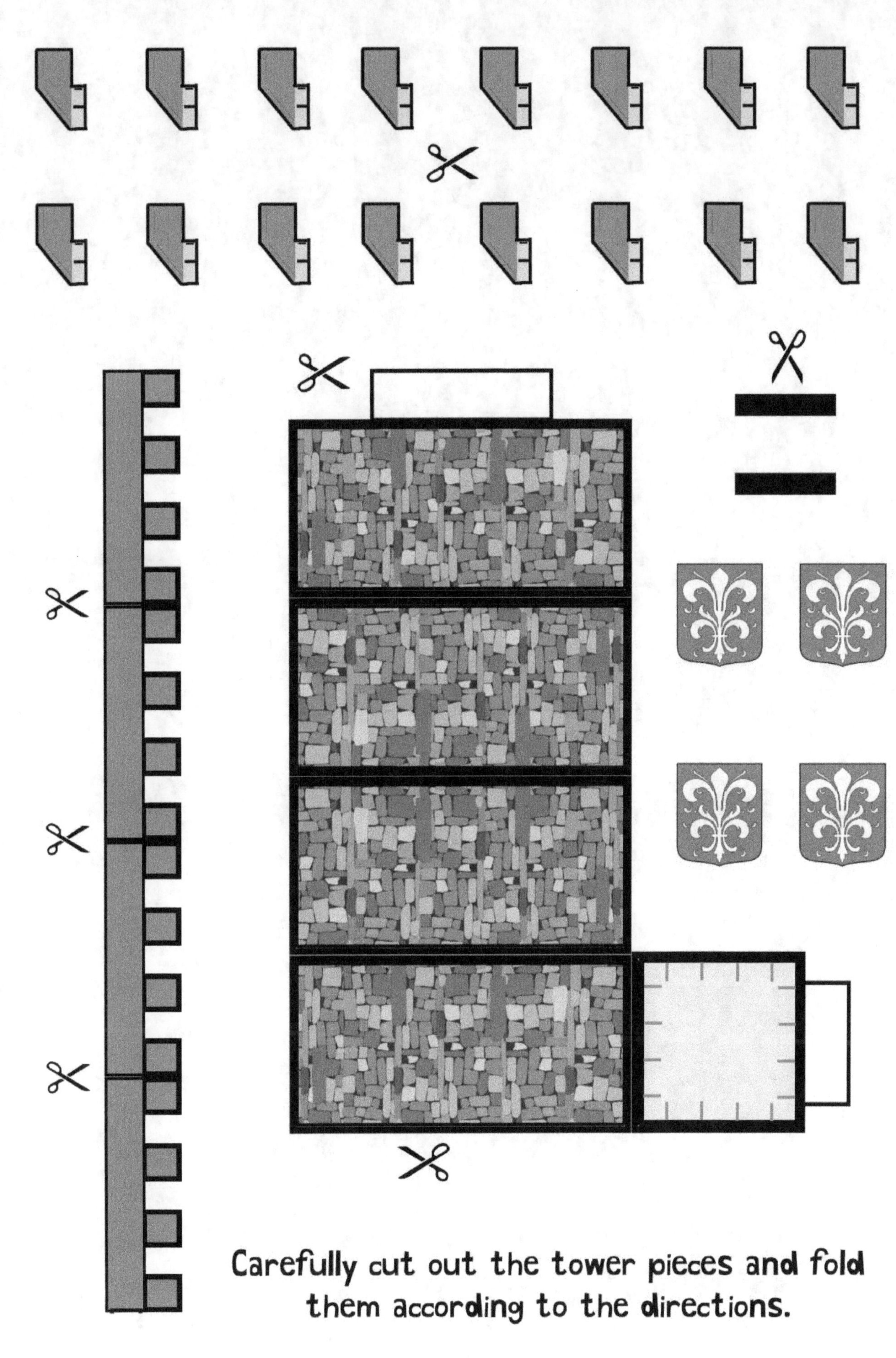

Carefully cut out the tower pieces and fold them according to the directions.

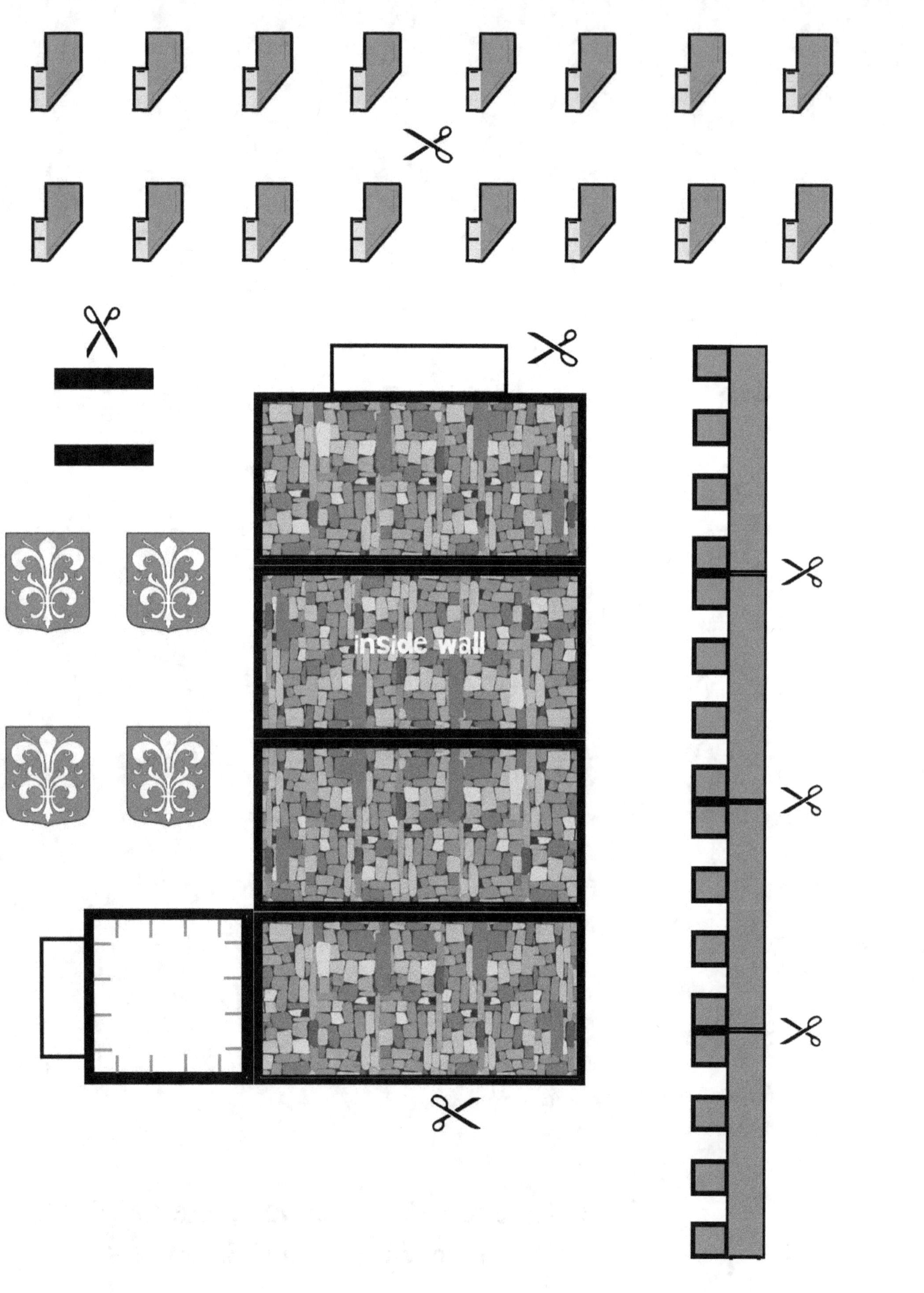

inside wall

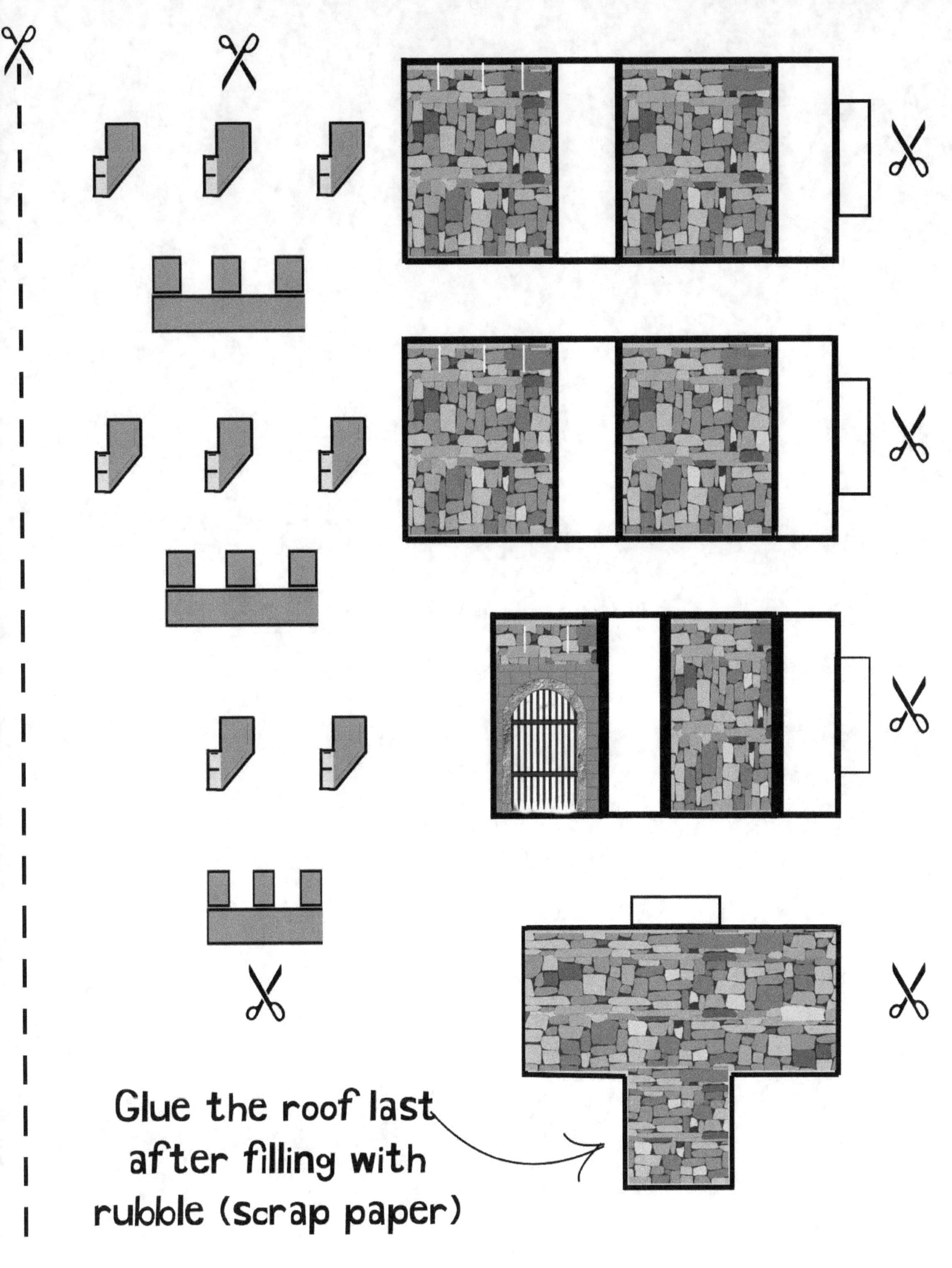

Glue the roof last
after filling with
rubble (scrap paper)

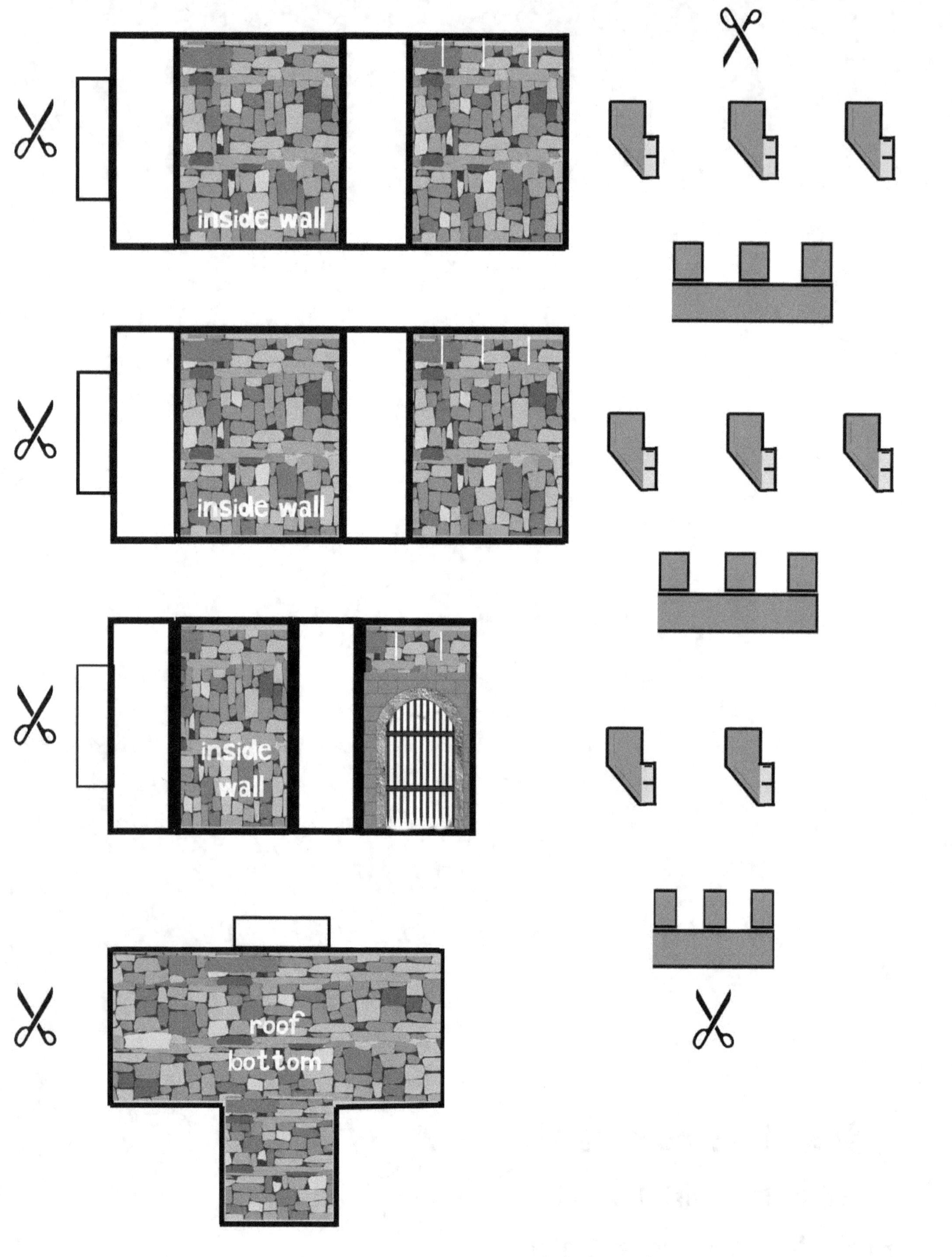

inside wall
inside wall
inside
wall
roof
bottom

1.

Cut out, fold & glue the two barbican towers the same as you did the corner towers.

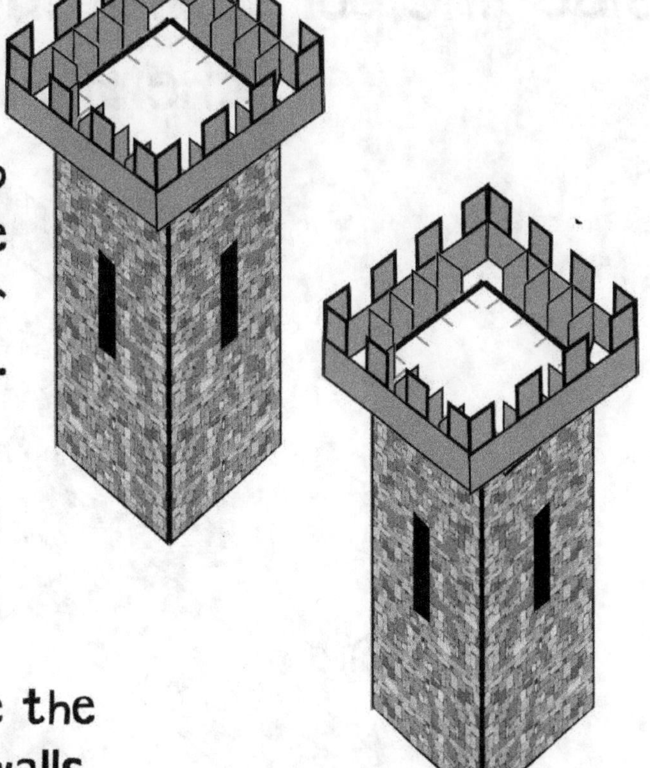

2. Cut out , fold & glue the barbican walls.

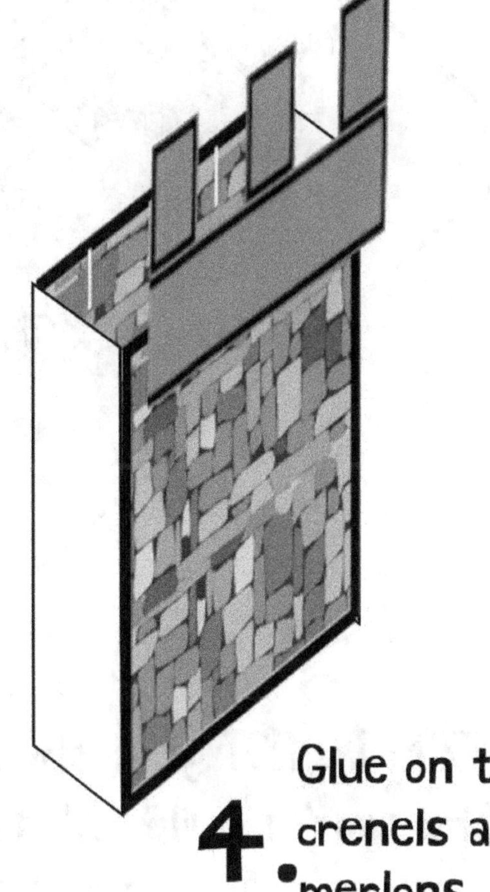

3. Glue the corbels on the white lines.

4. Glue on the crenels and merlons.

Glue the portcullis and the side walls of the barbican.

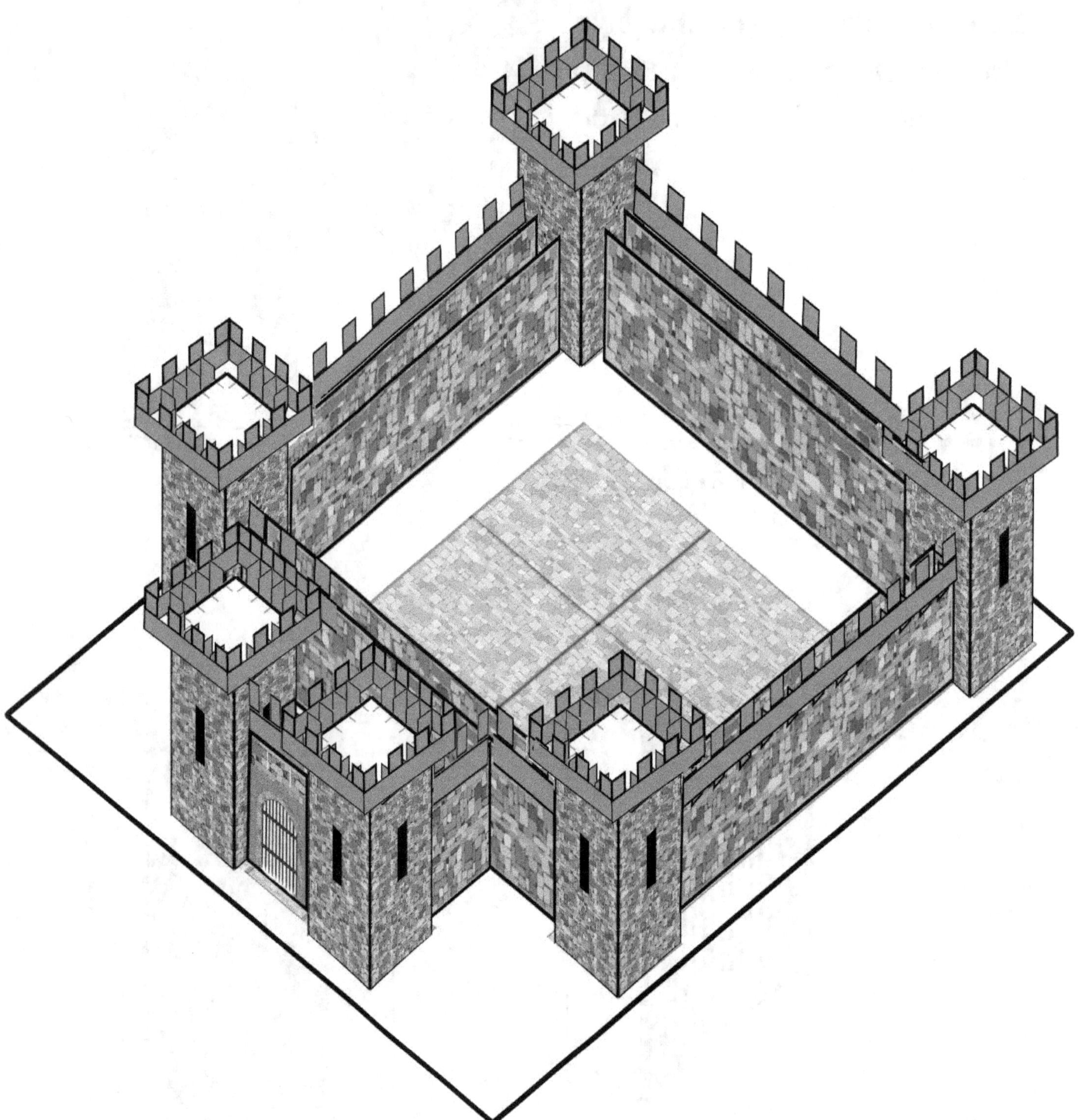

NOTE: DO NOT glue the walkway/roofs yet. At the end of the model build, fill the walls with rubble (scrap paper) and then glue the roofs on.

URGENT!!!

A siege is when a castle is to be taken over. The word siege comes from Latin and it means to sit. In a siege, the enemy will sit and wait, cutting off supplies to the castle and waiting for its occupants to surrender for lack of supplies and take it over.

A messenger has delivered a coded message to the king letting him know when the siege will happen so he can prepare. Can you break the code on the next page castle builder and find out when the siege will happen?

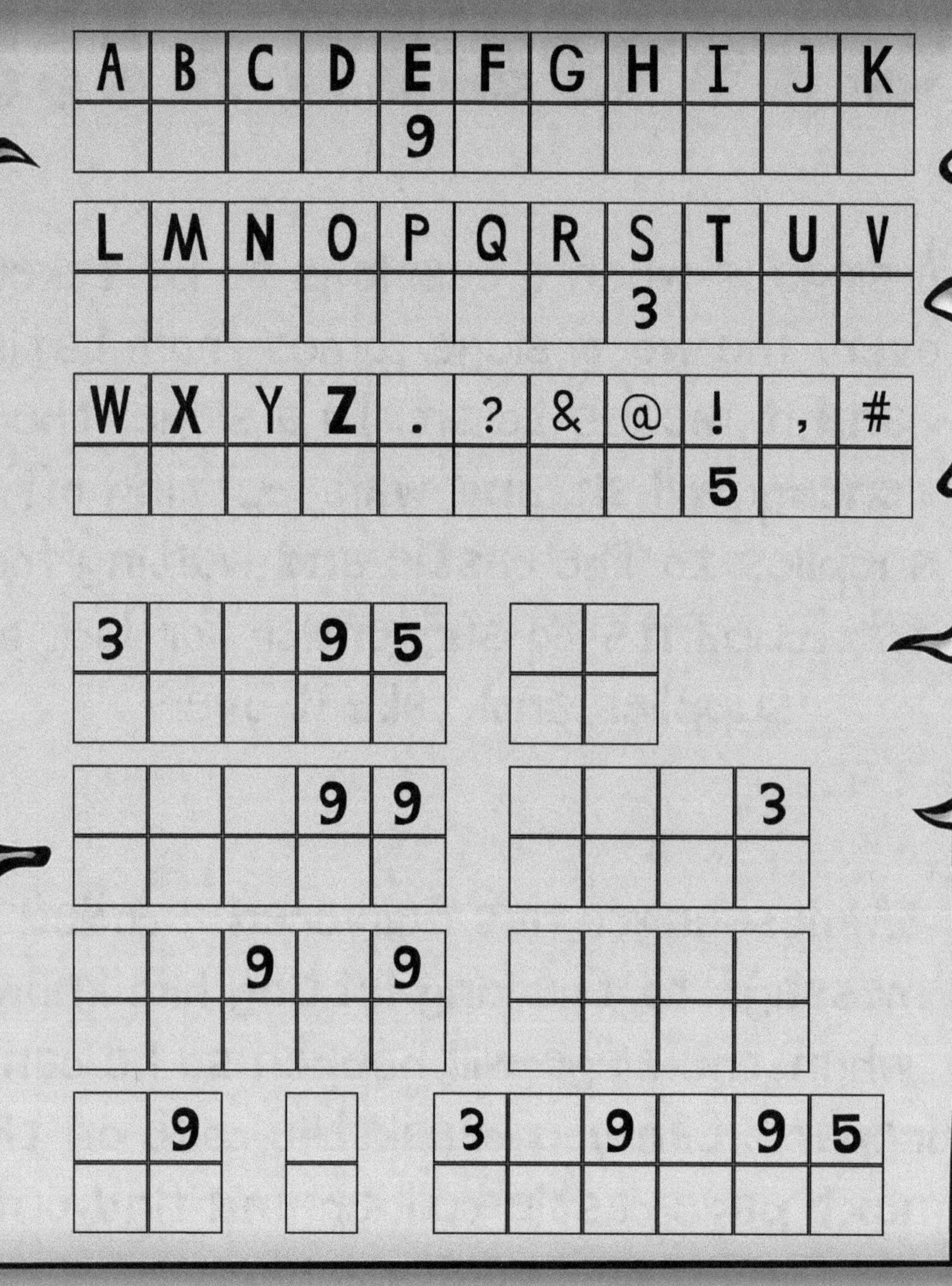

KEEP

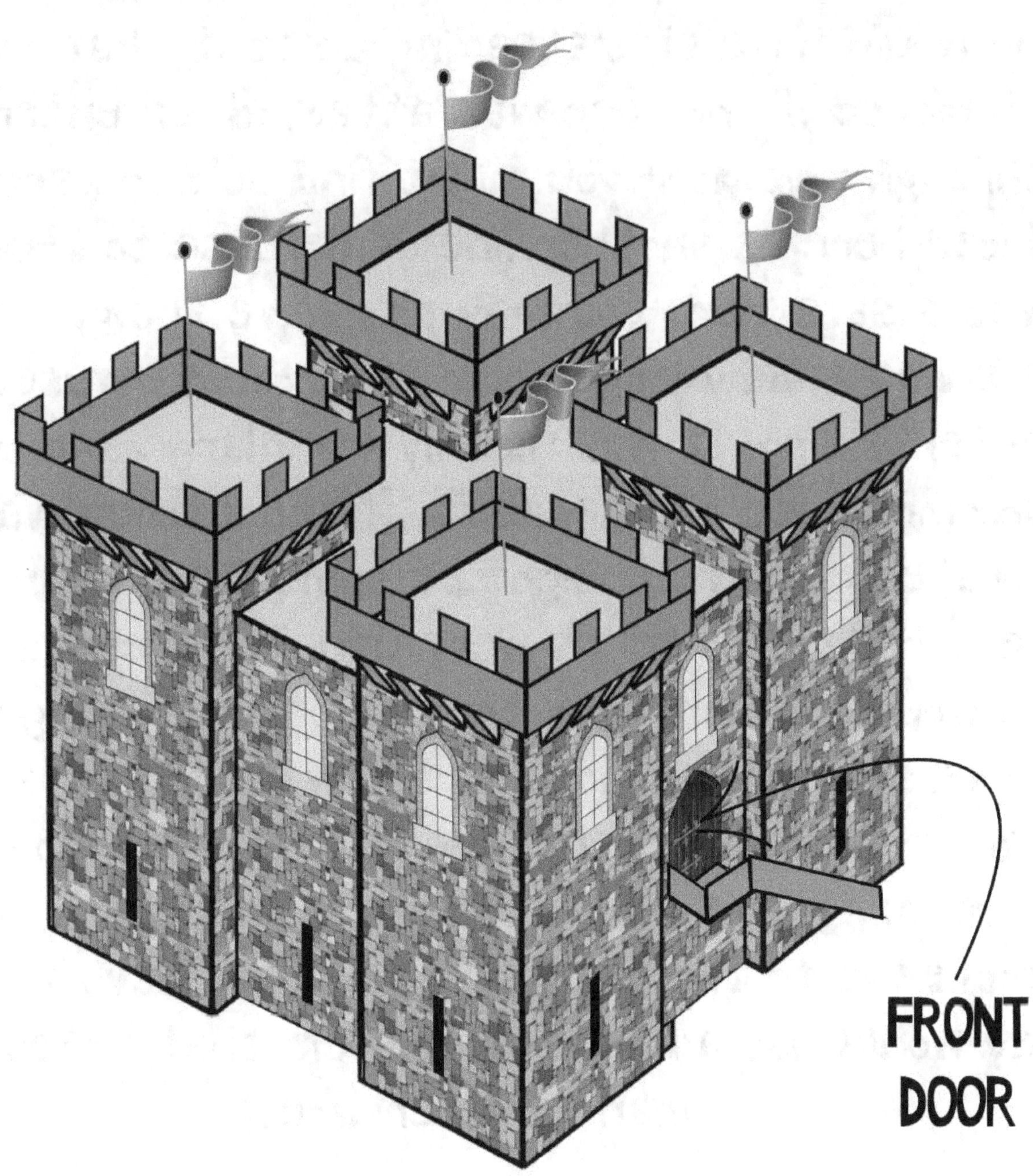

The keep would have been the safest place in the entire castle. It was the building where the castle owner and family might have their bedrooms on the top floor. The ground floor would usually be used as a storage area for supplies and sometimes a dungeon. The first floor (second floor in the USA) would be where one would enter the keep. The front door would have stairs leading up to it that could be removed if the keep was attacked. On entering through this door you might find soldier barracks placed here as another line of defense to keep the owners safe. Here you may also have the great hall. This was a very large room that could be used for entertaining. It was usually very large and could accommodate many guests. If the kitchen wasn't located outside it might be somewhere near the great hall. These keeps were usually several stories and would be built with the use of scaffolding where workers would put holes in the walls to put a wood beam in then add planks on top. As they moved up to the next level they simply removed the wood and moved it to the next story. To lift heavy things they would use a big pulley system that looked like a human hamster wheel.

GREAT HALL
BEDROOM
KITCHEN
STORAGE

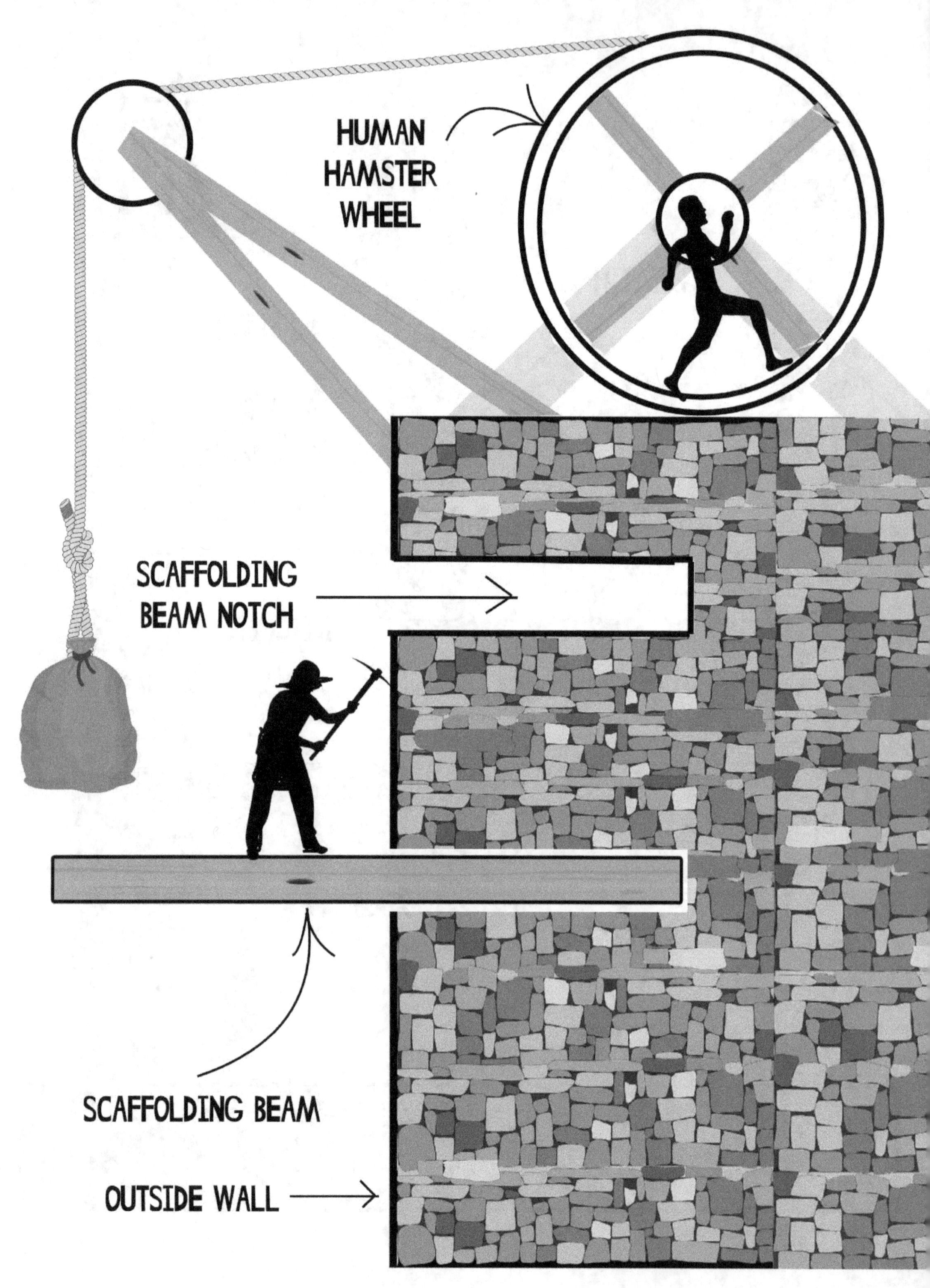

HUMAN
HAMSTER
WHEEL
SCAFFOLDING
BEAM NOTCH
SCAFFOLDING BEAM
OUTSIDE WALL

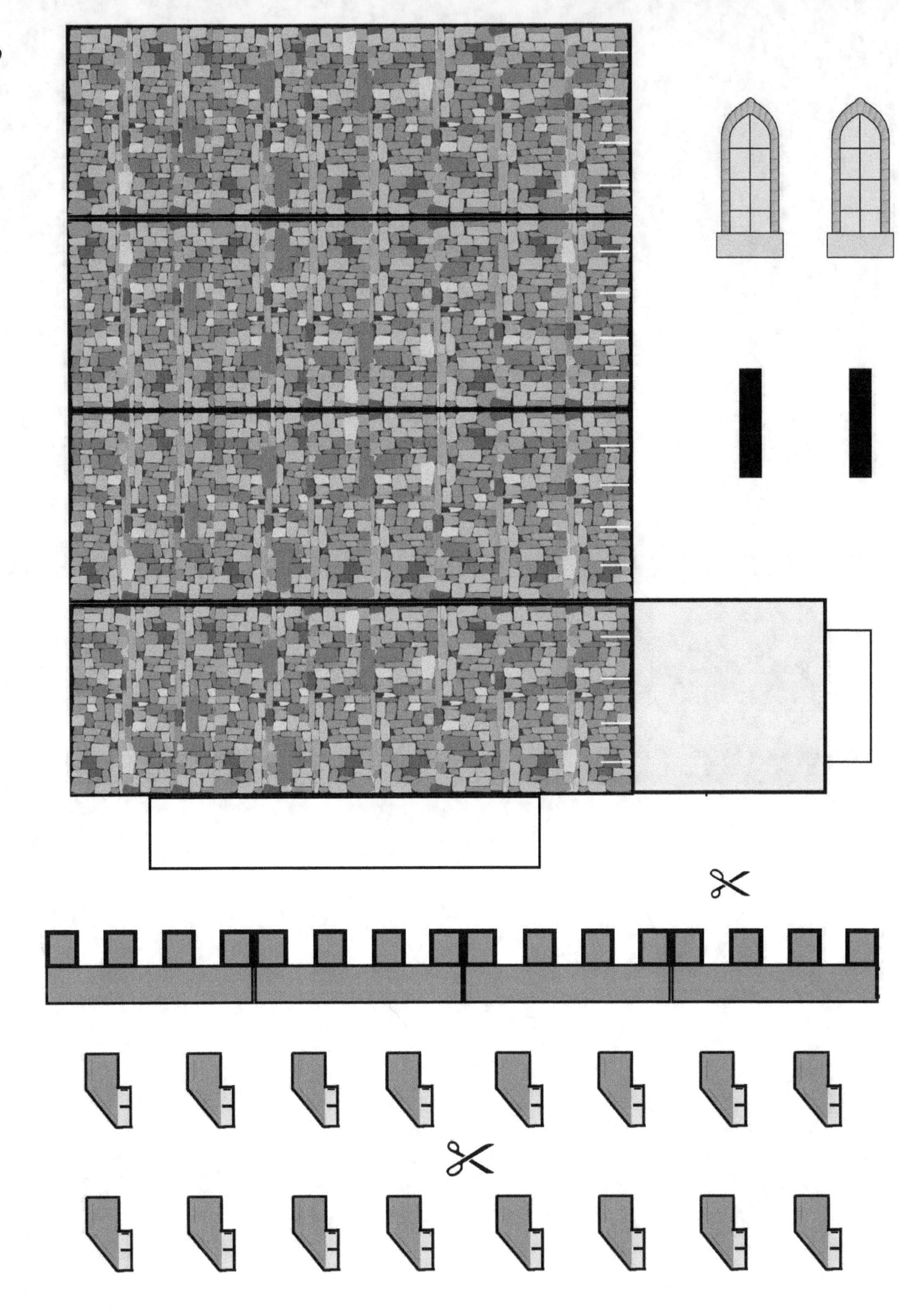

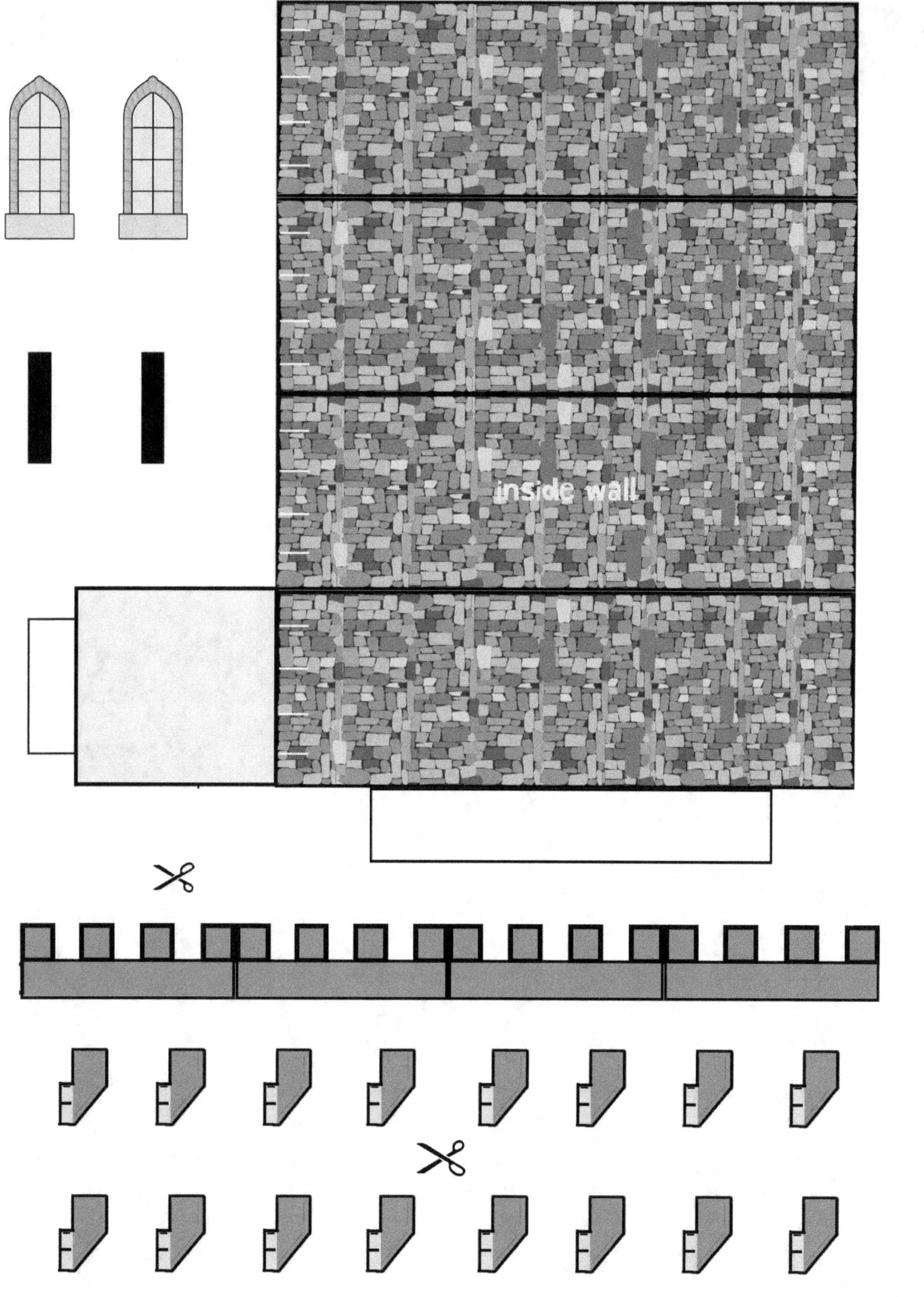

inside wall

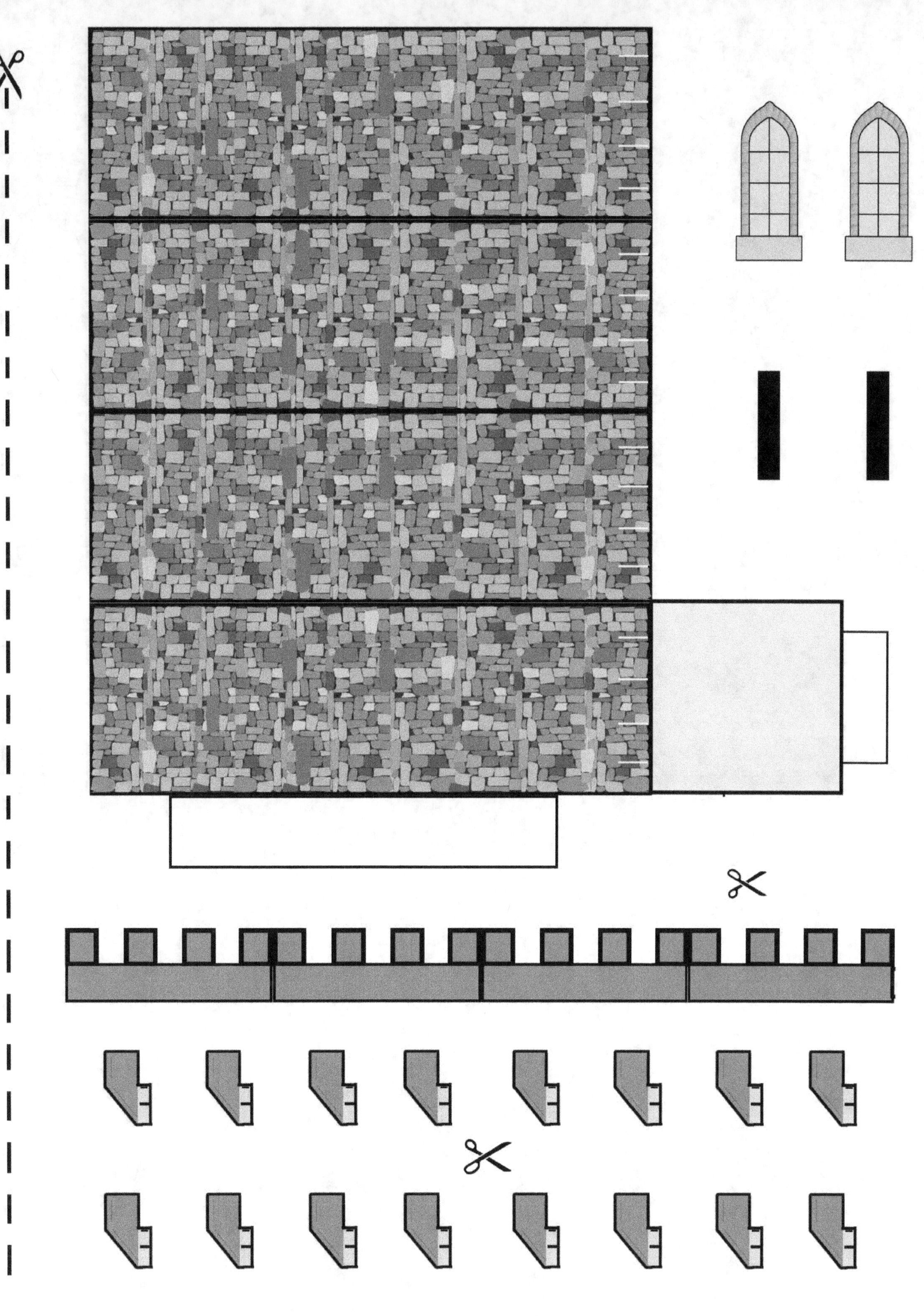

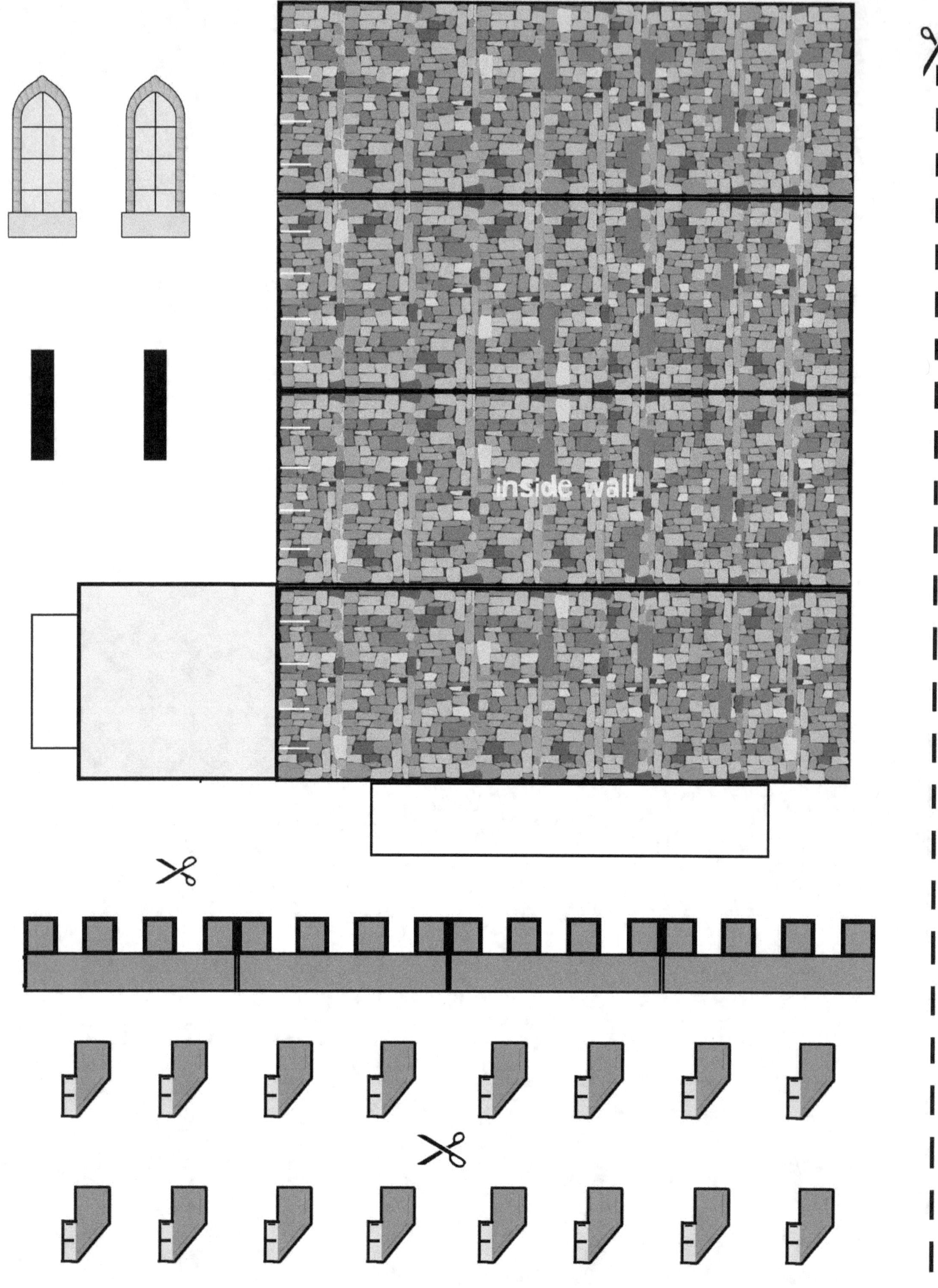
inside wall

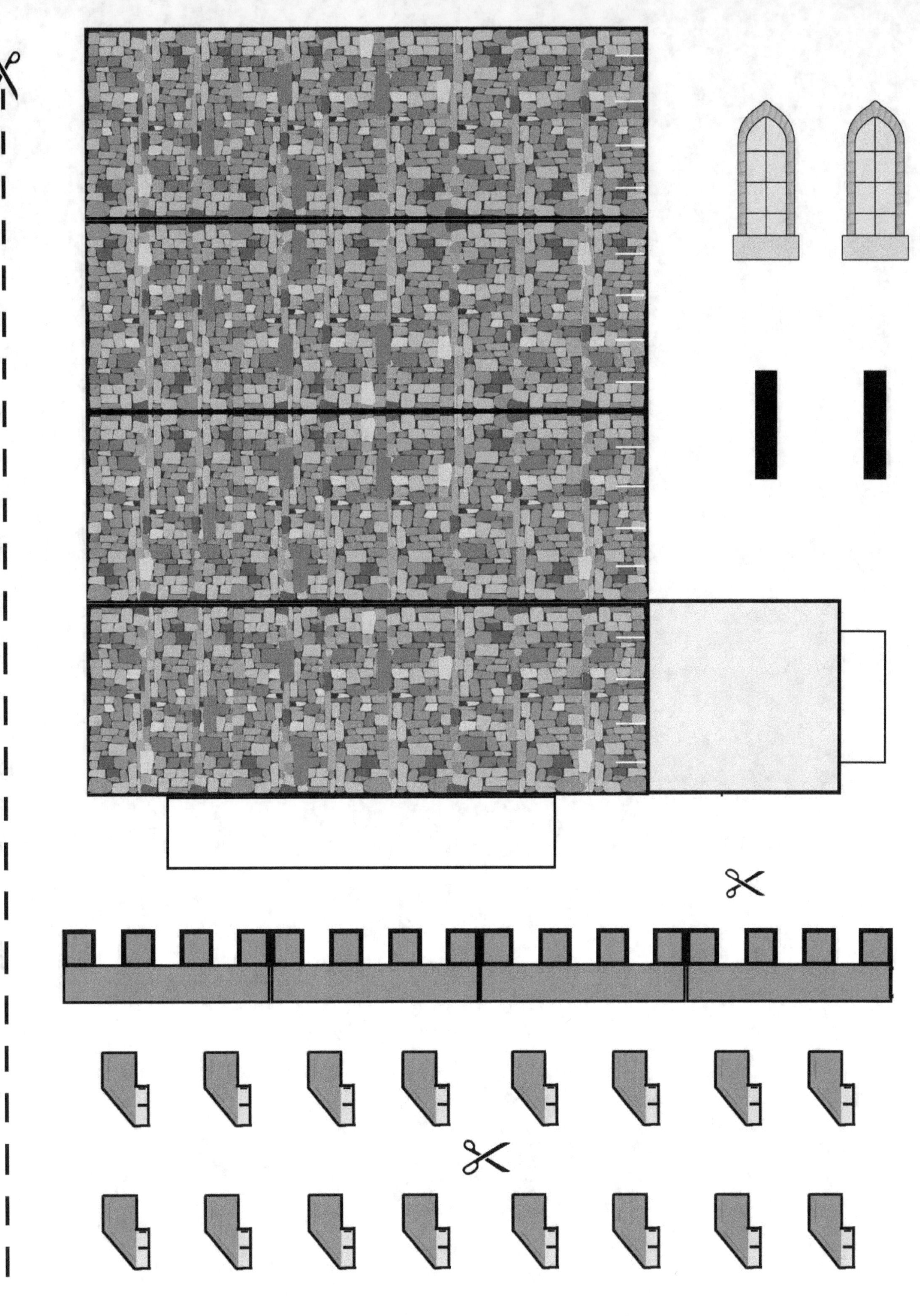

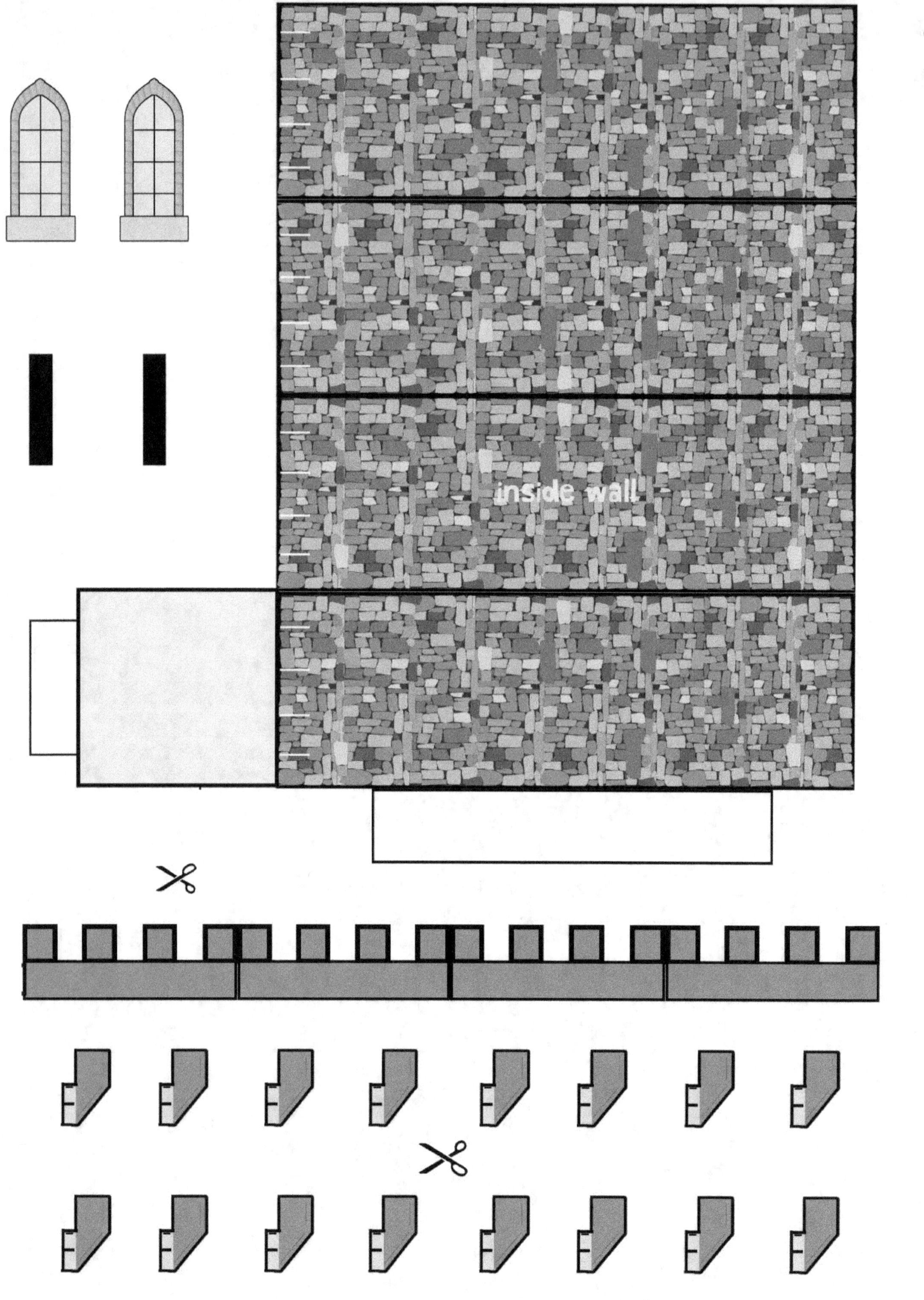

inside wall

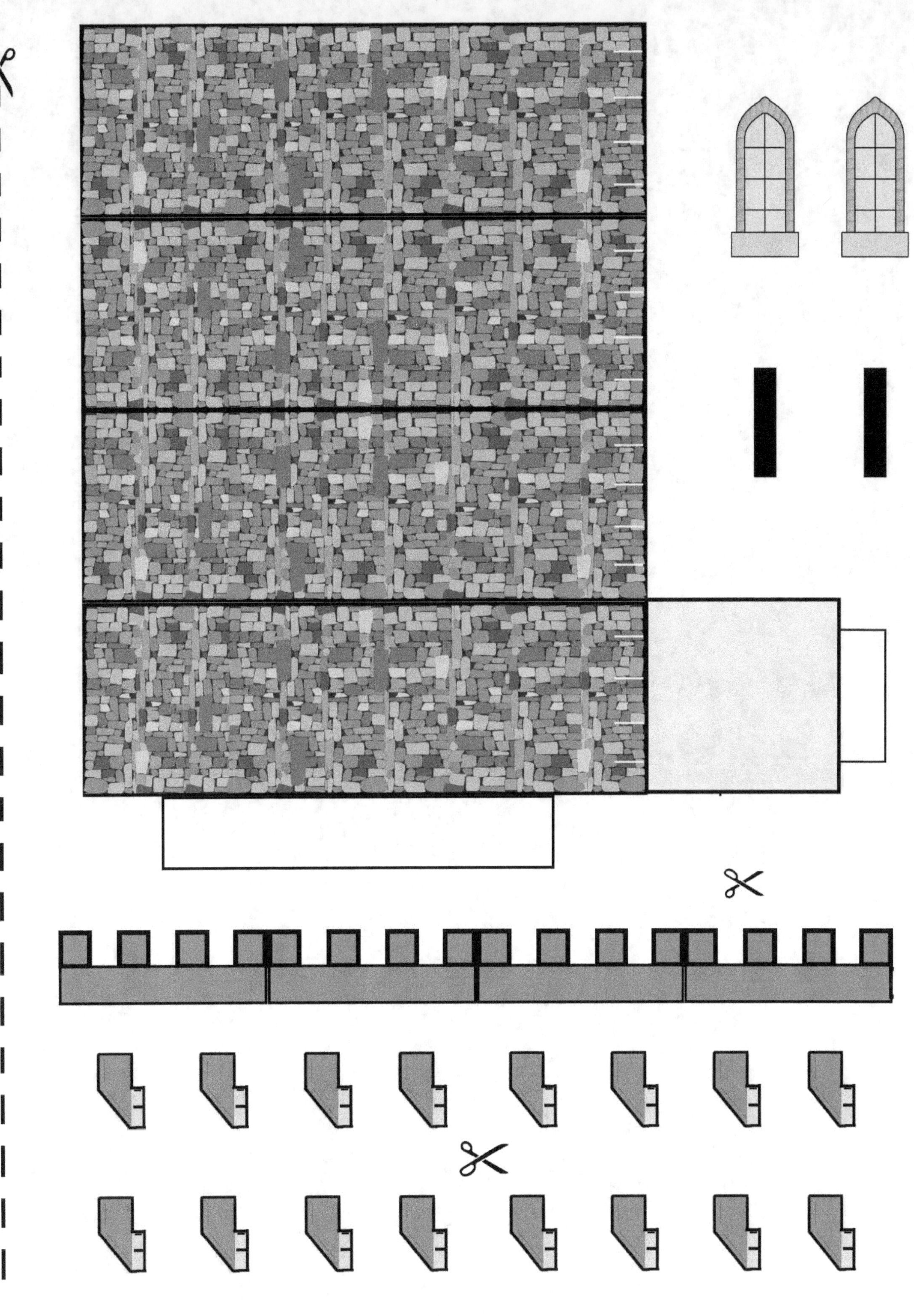

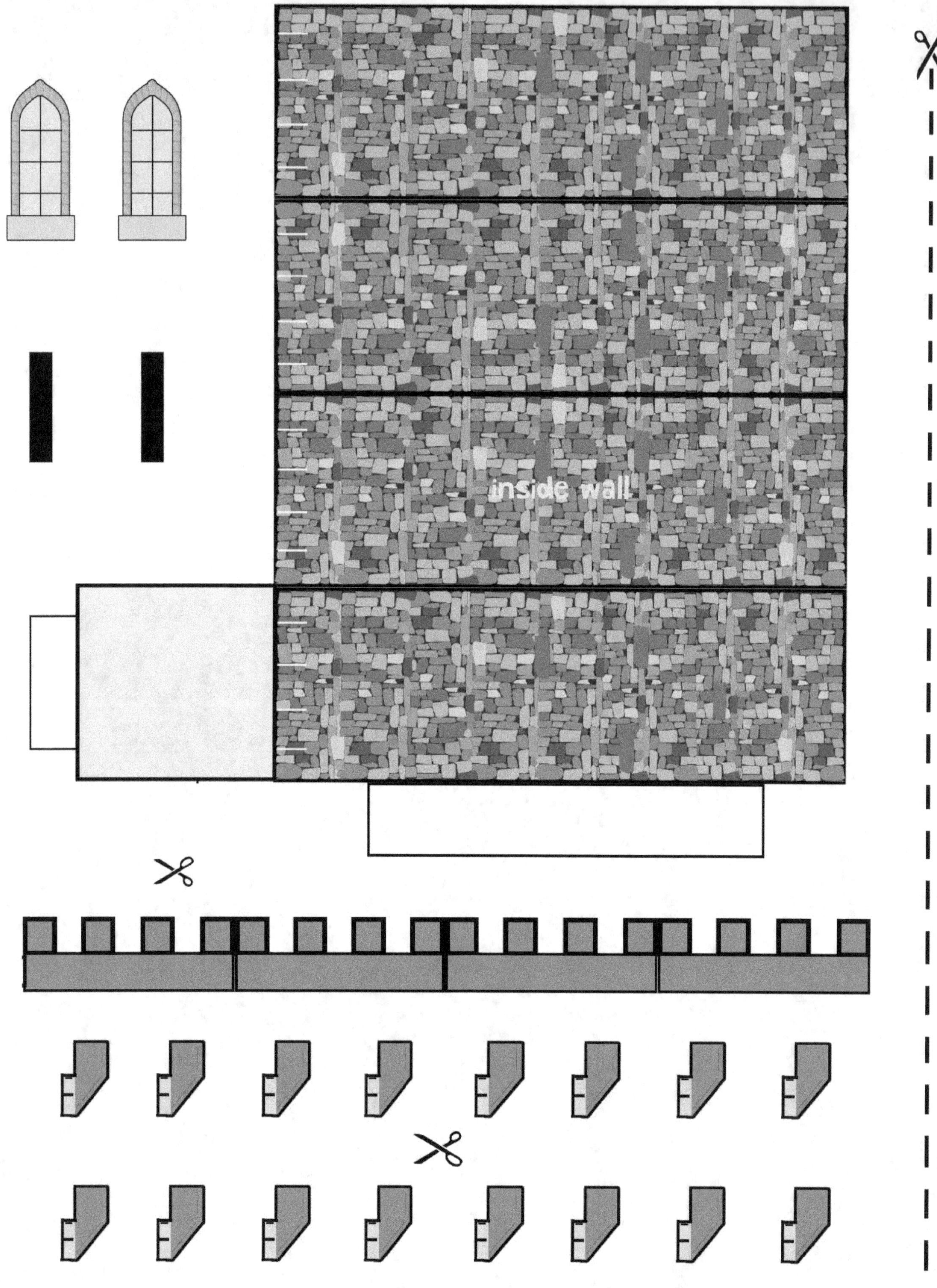

inside wall

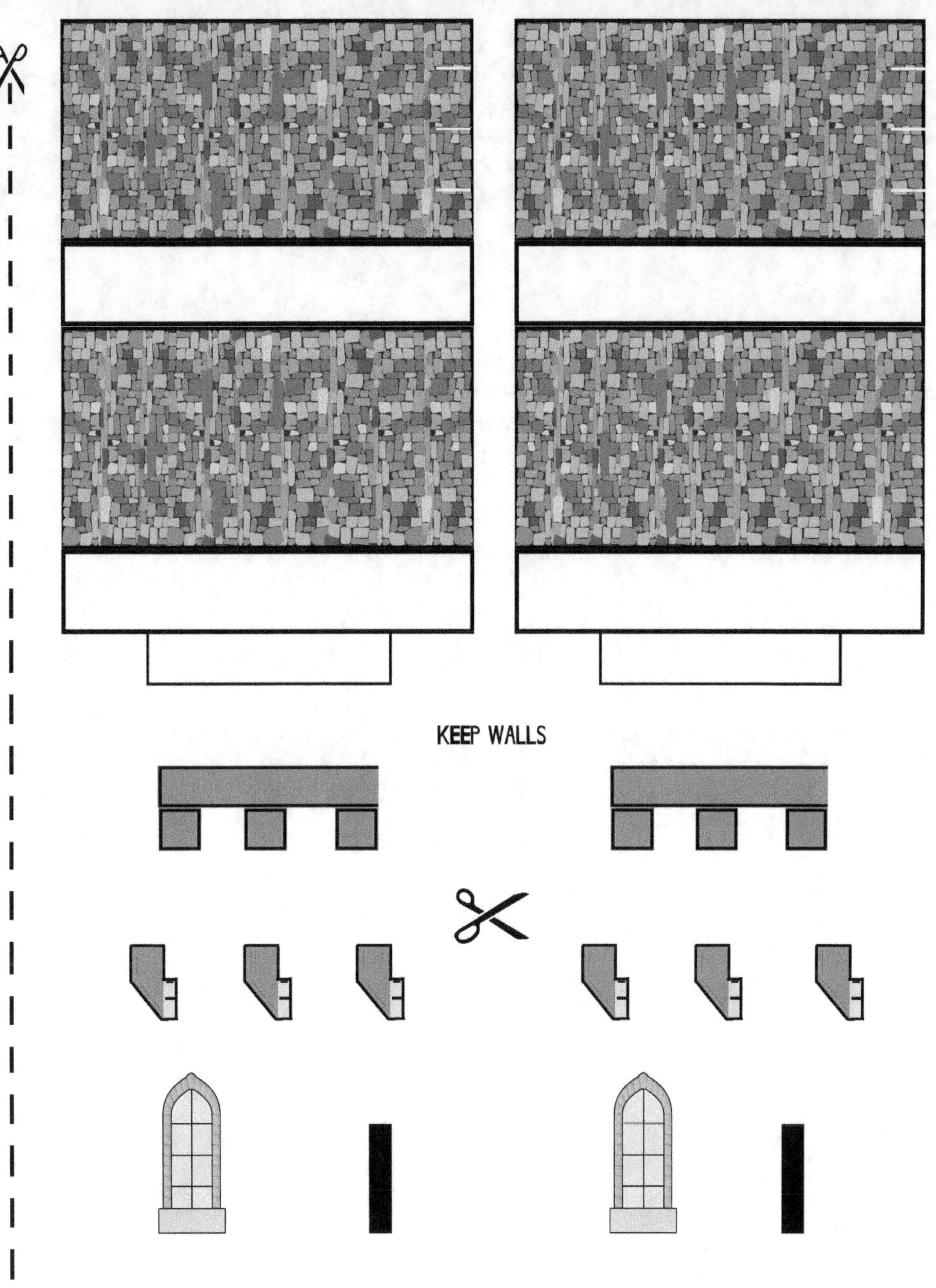

KEEP WALLS

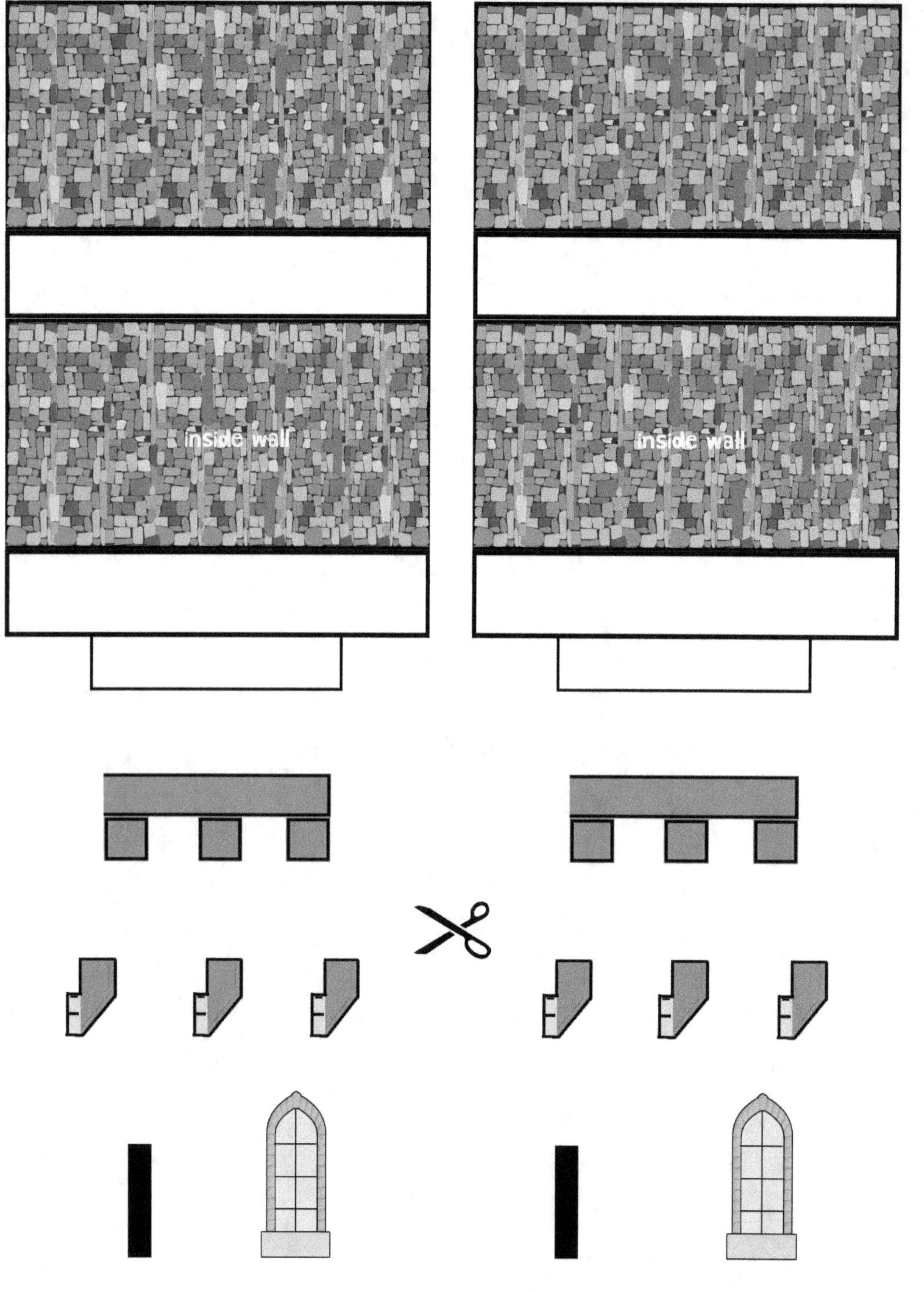

inside wall
inside wall

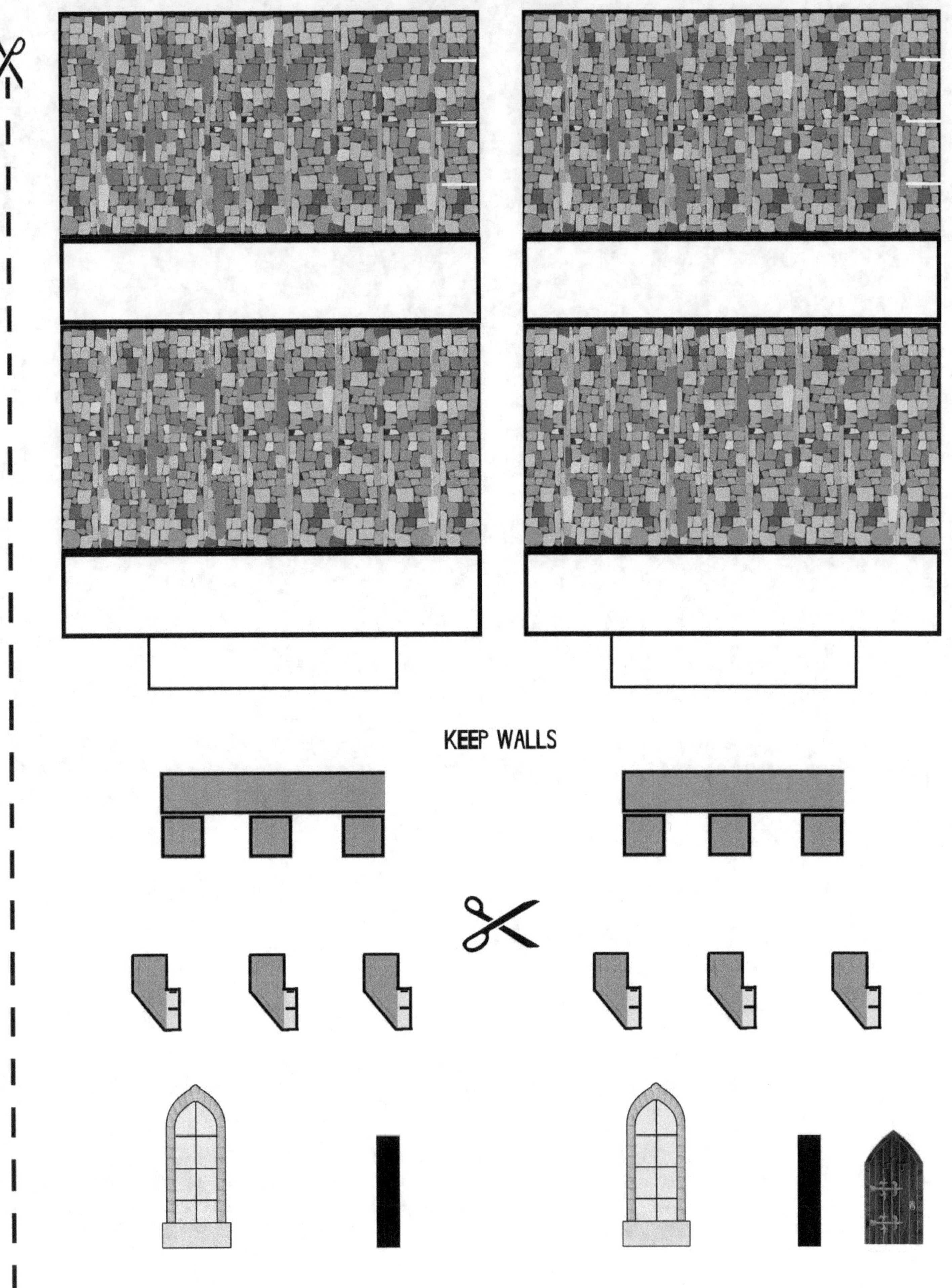

KEEP WALLS

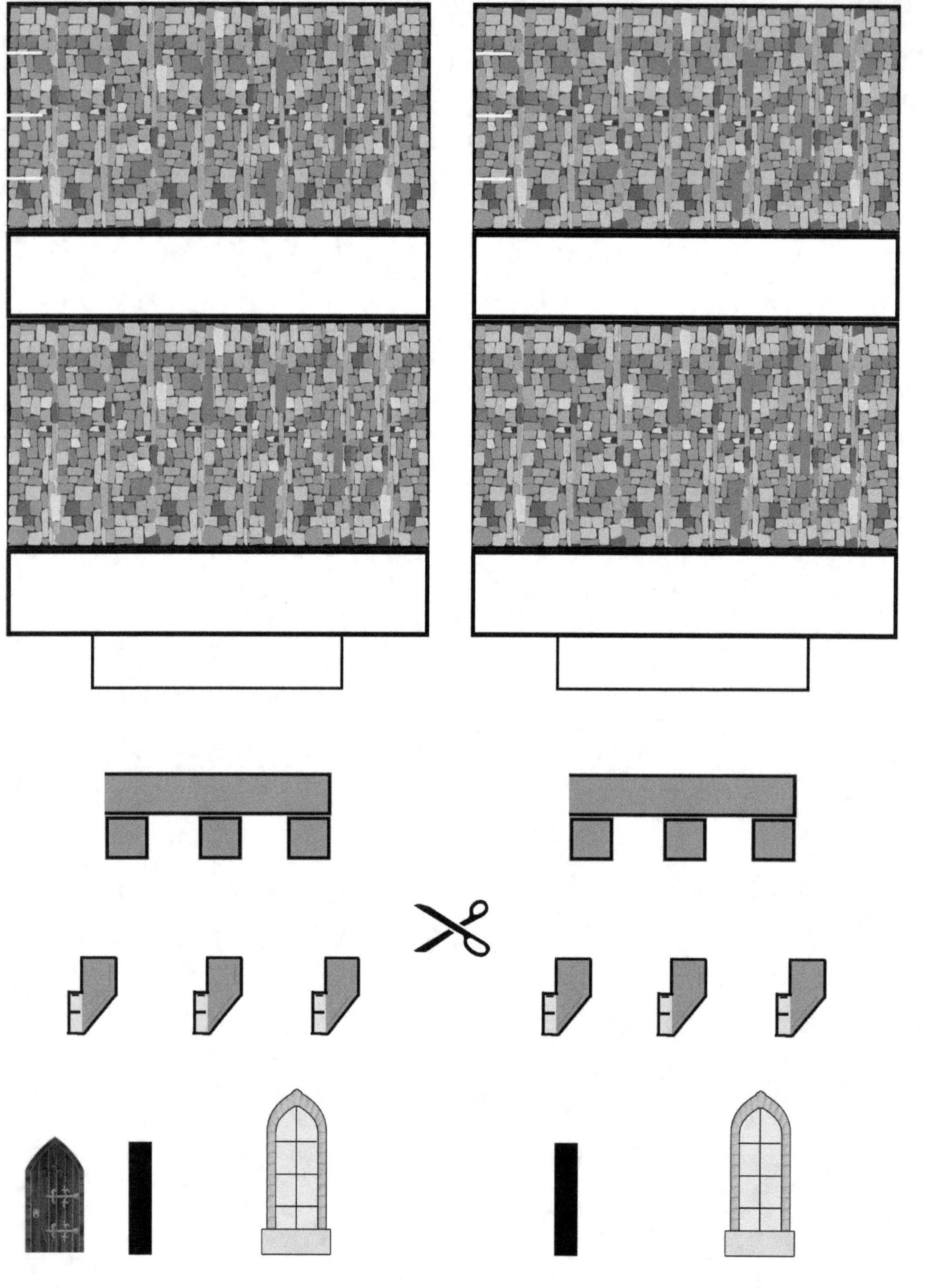

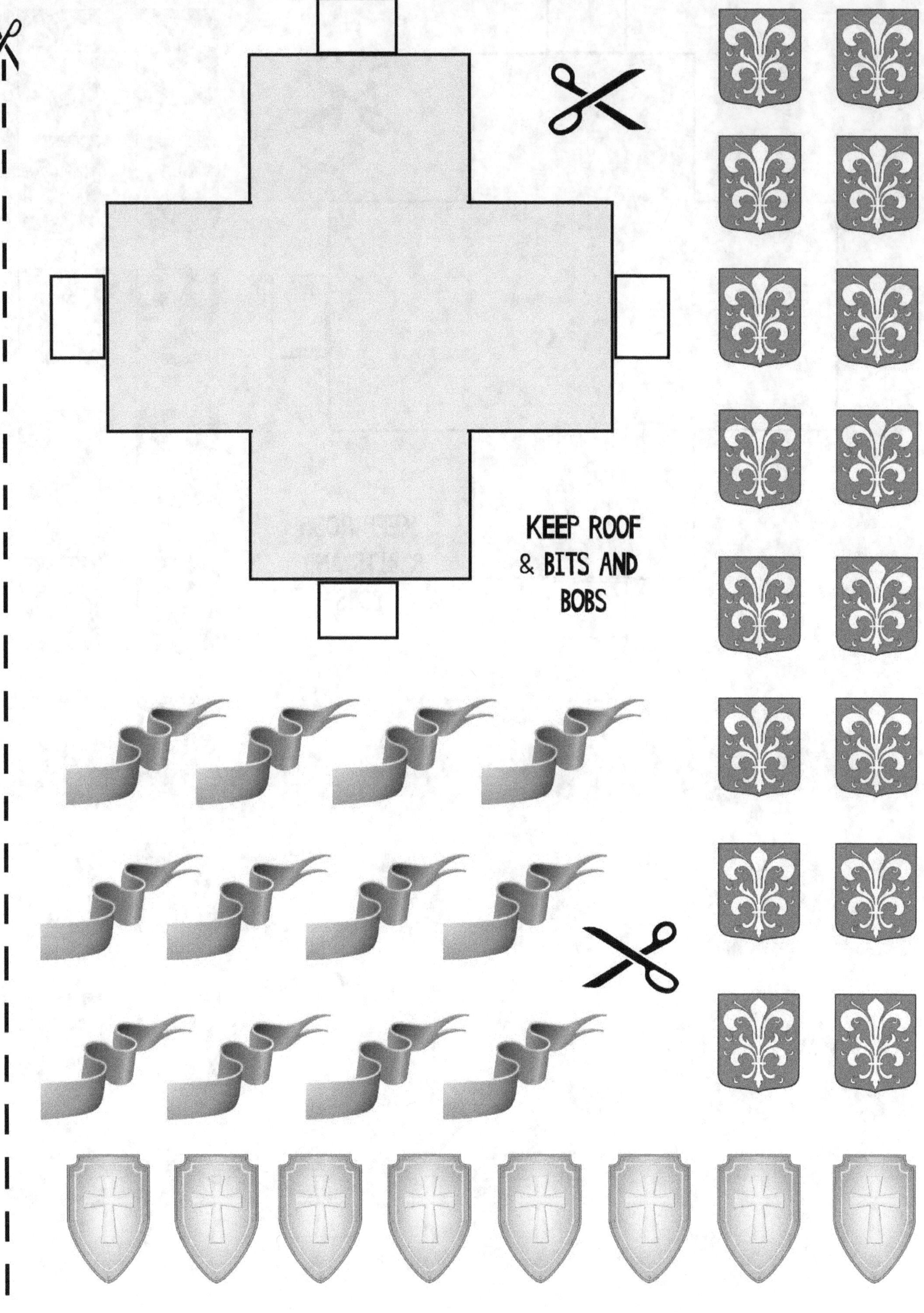

KEEP ROOF
& BITS AND
BOBS

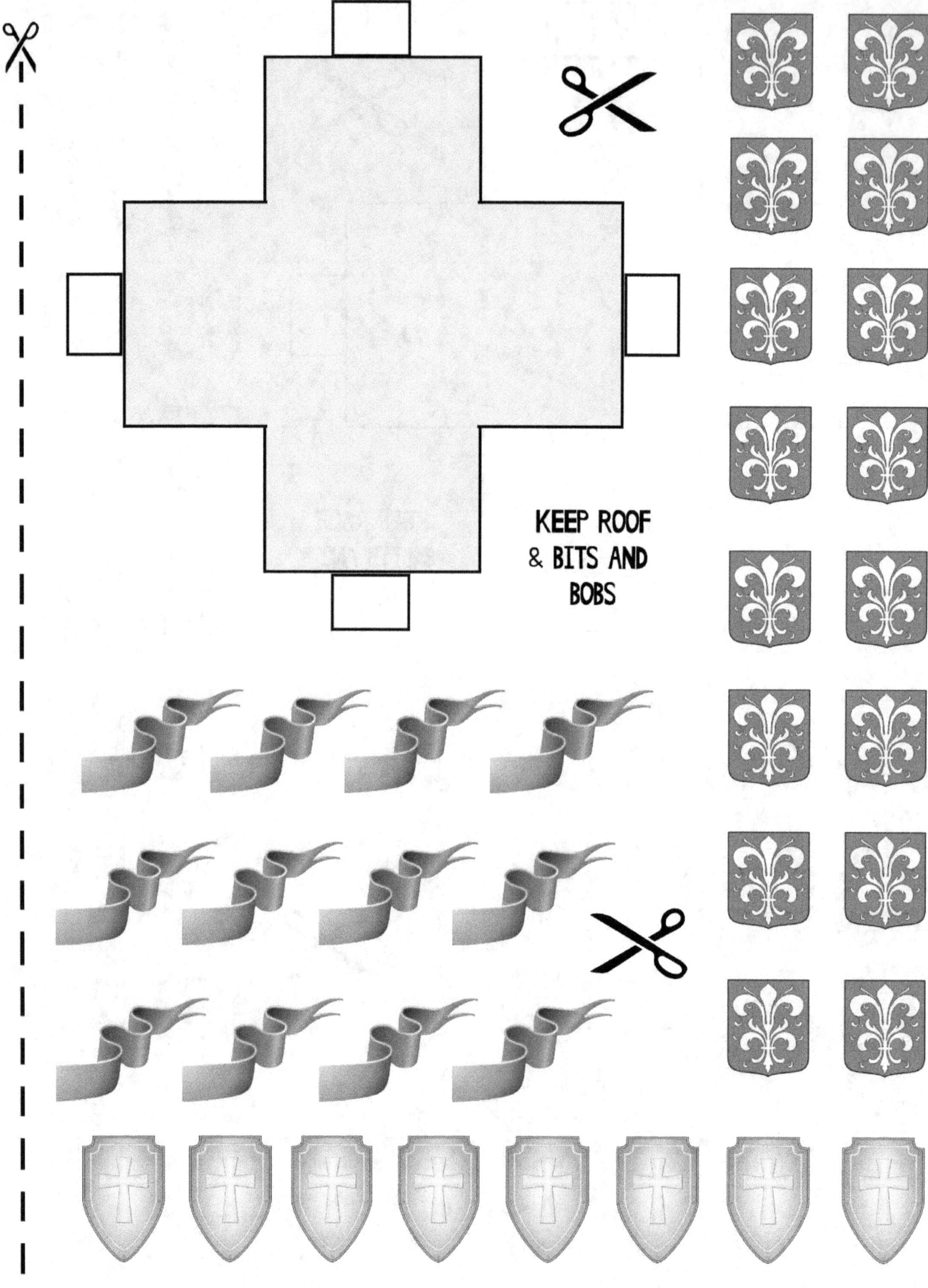
KEEP ROOF
& BITS AND
BOBS

1.

Cut out, fold & glue the four keep towers the same as you did the corner towers.

2. Cut out , fold & glue the keep walls.

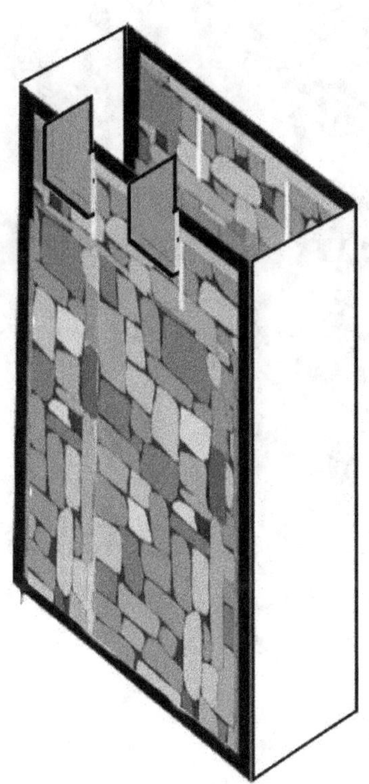

3. Glue the corbels on the white lines.

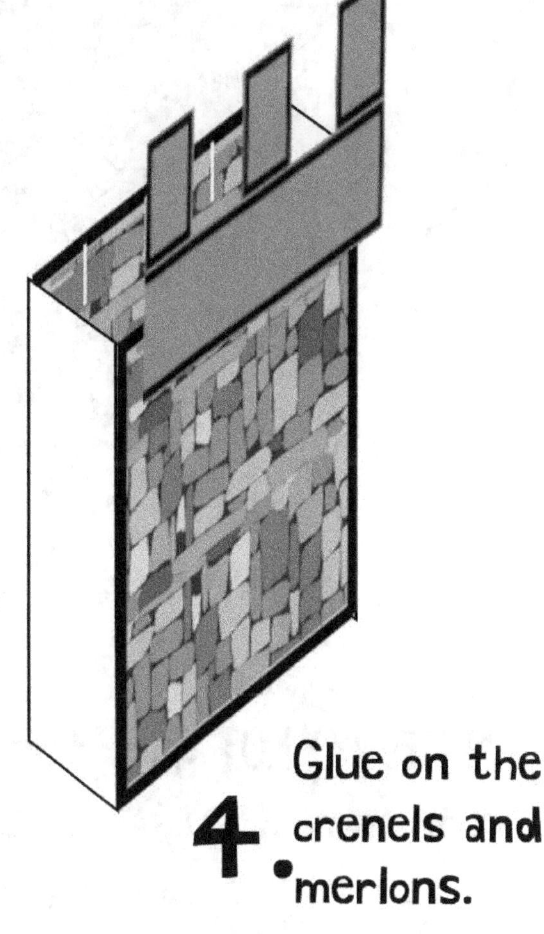

Glue on the crenels and merlons.

4.

Glue the keep walls to the keep towers and then glue the whole keep to the base.

NOTE: DO NOT glue the walkway/roofs yet. At the end of the model build, fill the walls with rubble (scrap paper) and then glue the roofs on.

Grendel the Dragon has been terrorizing the castle. The king has sent Sir Garfunkel to slay him. Help Sir Garfunkel find his way through Grendel's lair.

CASTLE PARTS WORD SCRAMBLE

1. A secret door.
   O T S E R P N   _ _ _ _ _ _ _

2. A water-filled trench.
   T M A O   _ _ _ _

3. The castle's courtyard.
   I Y B E A L   _ _ _ _ _ _

4. The castle's safest building.
   E K P E   _ _ _ _

5. The outside wall between towers.
   R L C N I U L W A T A

   _ _ _ _ _ _ _ _ _ _ _

GARDEROBE

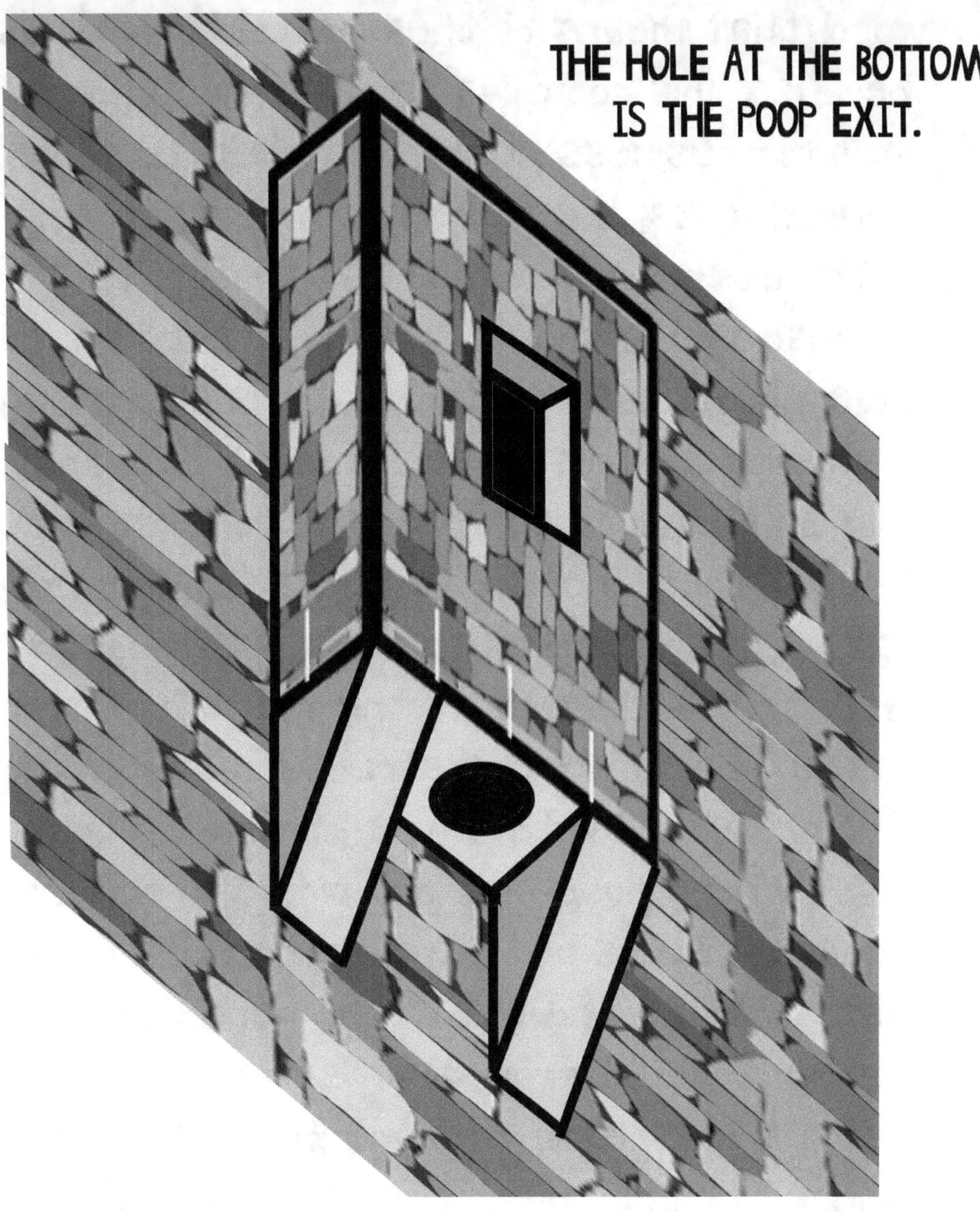

Well, castle builder, you have probably been wondering where people poop in a castle. The answer is the garderobe. This is a French word that means clothes protector. That's because this room was a place not only to do your business but also a place to store your clothes, like a closet. The reason why the clothes were in the bathroom was because the ammonia smell was thought to have killed fleas in clothing (bugs in clothing in medieval times were common). Now they didn't have flush toilets back then so basically there were two places for the poop to go, in the moat (or the outside castle wall) or in a cesspit at the bottom of the castle. The garderobe structure stuck out from the wall with a hole at the bottom. This is where poop and pee would drop down several stories onto the ground or in the moat. LOOK OUT BELOW!!! If the garderobe was inside it would drop down several stories into a cesspit which some poor servant would routinely have to clean out. GROSS!!!

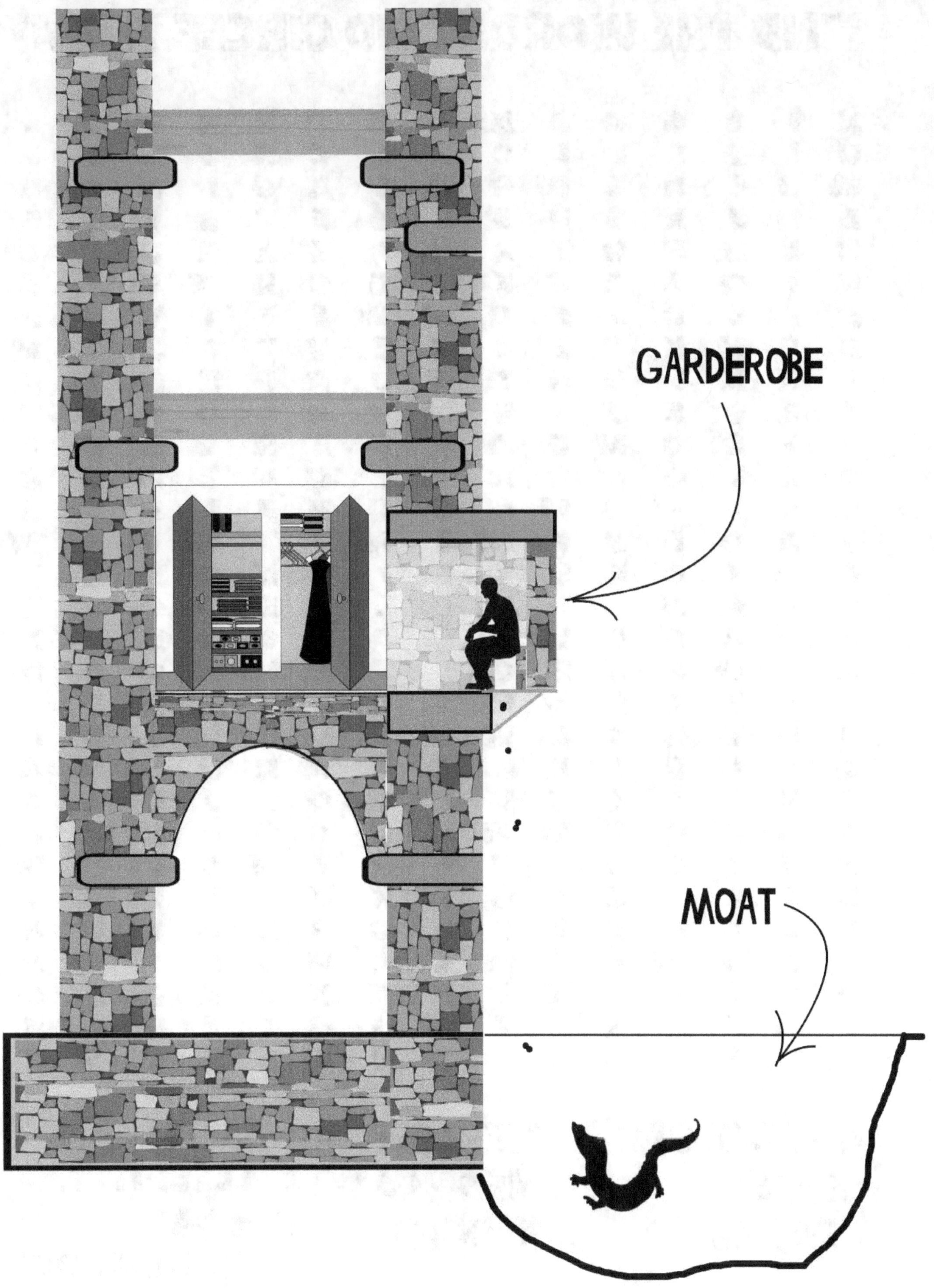

GARDEROBE
MOAT

FIND THE WORDS AND CIRCLE THEM!

X	I	B	G	Q	A	K	O	B	P	H	X	P	S	L
U	L	J	S	F	L	C	Z	L	C	R	E	N	E	L
W	Z	E	H	Z	P	R	R	D	K	G	I	N	T	B
D	H	J	X	S	R	S	I	B	E	V	K	W	J	S
N	L	U	P	R	T	X	K	I	Z	X	H	U	D	O
M	F	Q	A	A	P	E	S	G	U	H	M	Y	F	G
E	I	L	O	J	F	Q	M	W	E	F	T	V	J	P
D	B	M	K	Y	E	Z	V	E	V	T	I	J	W	M
I	K	N	I	G	H	T	K	D	R	P	K	R	Y	R
E	B	B	X	J	J	V	M	V	H	L	D	Q	N	U
V	V	R	Q	M	G	A	R	D	E	R	O	B	E	D
A	C	L	O	U	B	R	W	F	Q	H	Z	N	R	R
L	V	Y	W	B	M	C	U	H	H	A	B	Y	D	A
J	A	Q	G	B	K	M	Z	M	Y	Z	U	V	A	W
Q	N	K	C	E	S	S	P	I	T	K	Q	H	K	B
P	I	M	N	O	N	B	I	L	A	R	Q	G	X	R
K	D	W	D	E	Y	W	C	A	N	O	X	S	X	I
N	S	W	I	K	E	C	I	R	E	H	N	Q	D	D
R	R	S	O	P	M	R	W	U	V	S	A	D	Q	G
R	D	Y	H	C	Q	W	U	U	L	K	V	J	B	E
Q	P	M	B	Y	F	E	G	D	D	R	H	F	B	G
S	H	P	O	G	U	L	P	Q	G	I	J	L	A	D
N	N	H	Q	D	M	W	X	U	O	G	I	K	X	Z
M	J	Y	G	D	L	V	F	R	Z	M	C	L	U	M
B	A	A	Y	G	G	G	I	K	K	T	I	E	C	O
L	A	O	N	A	U	X	L	O	R	D	O	T	U	N
I	D	G	W	I	G	W	K	Q	H	V	K	I	W	D
O	I	Z	V	C	K	L	P	K	K	U	A	P	J	Q
F	A	G	J	A	F	T	M	J	O	C	Z	R	Q	K
E	R	F	T	Q	K	Y	P	B	E	U	T	L	M	K

GARDEROBE
SIEGE
CRENEL

MERLON
MEDIEVAL
KNIGHT

LORD
CESSPIT
MOAT
DRAWBRIDGE

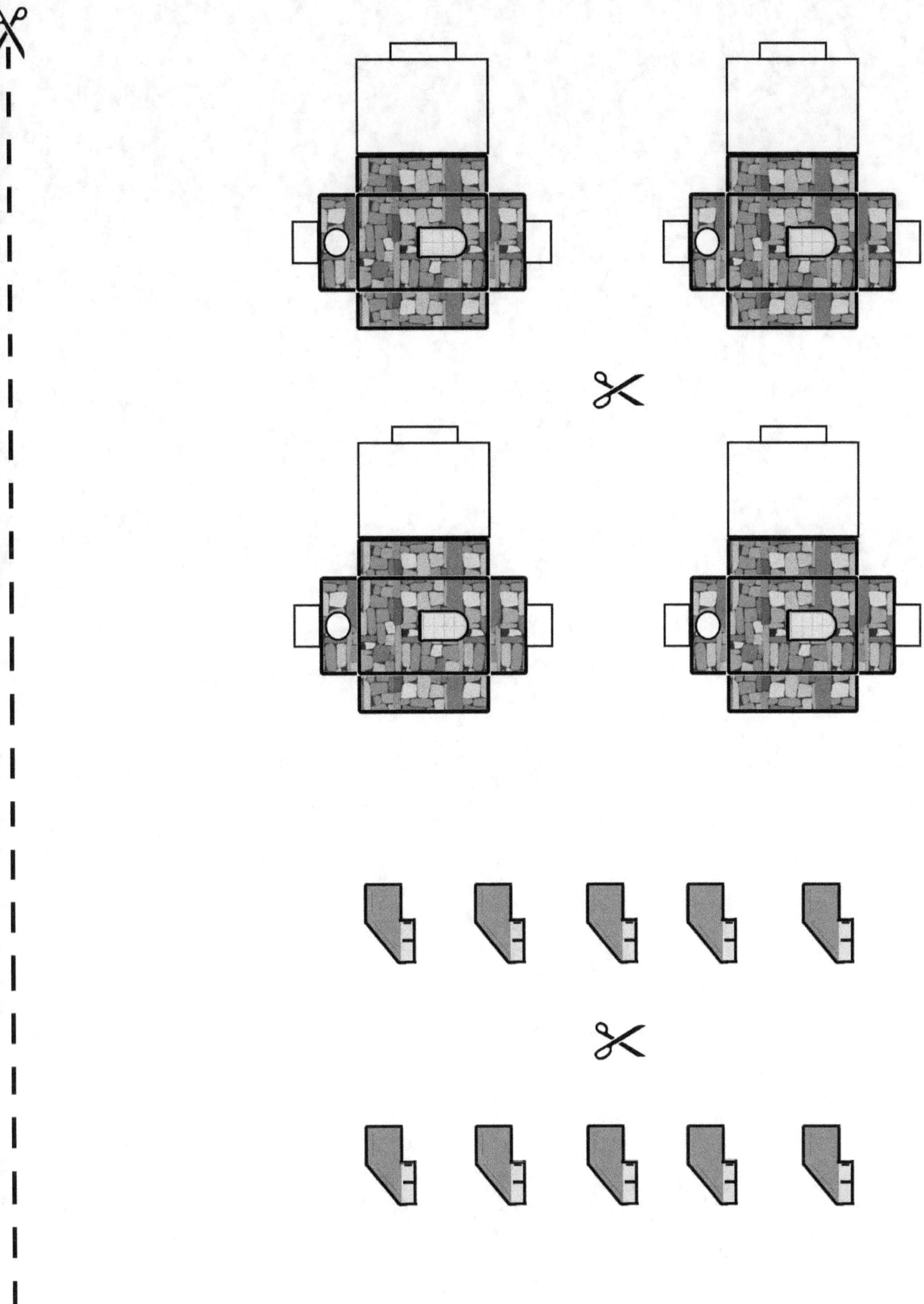

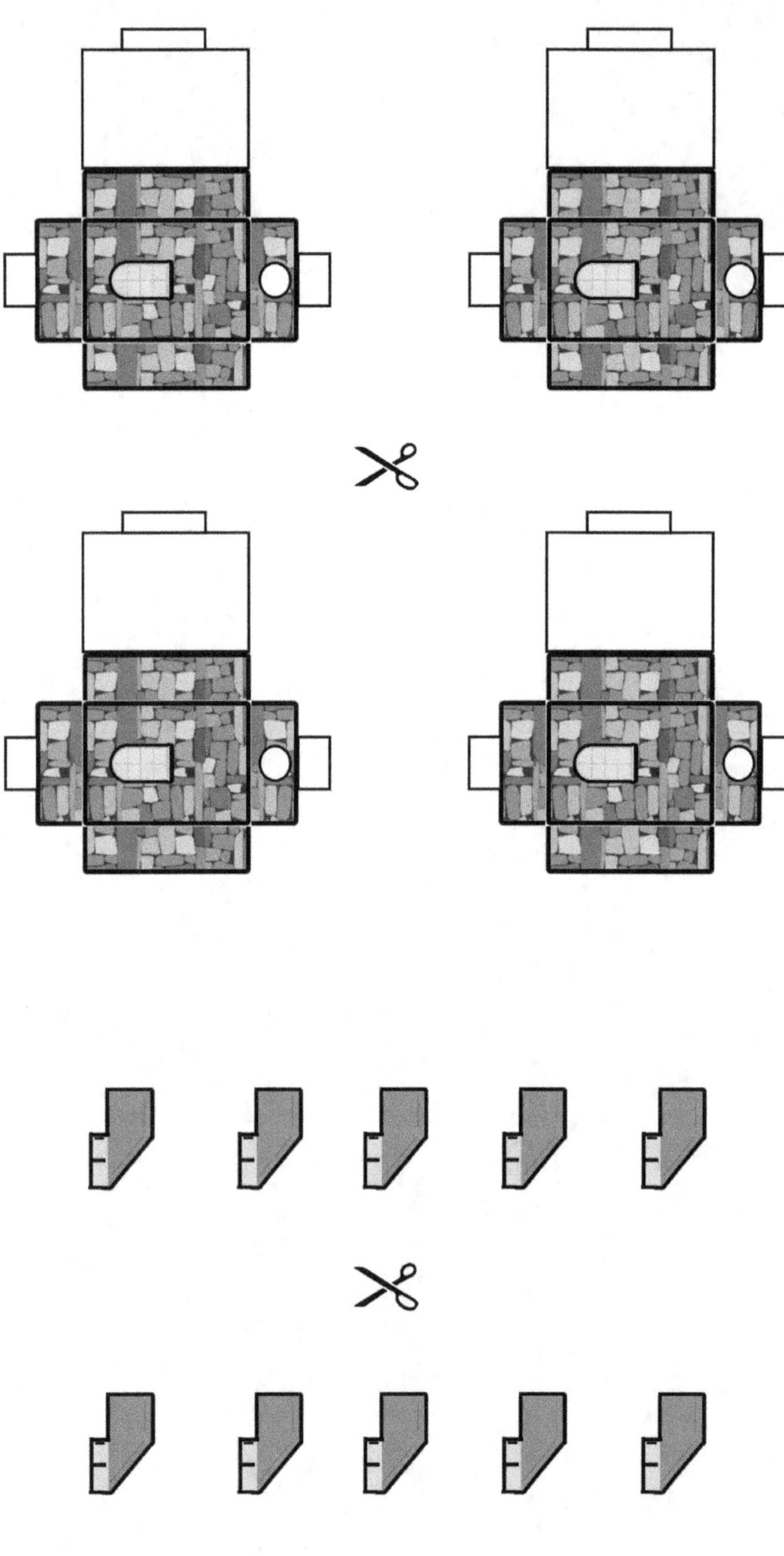

1.

Cut out the four garderobes and fold and glue them into a box shape like this.

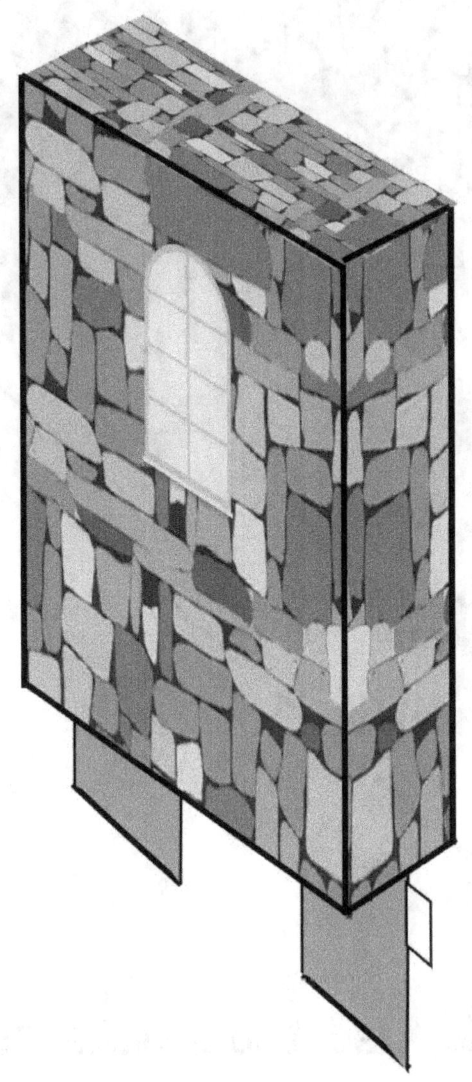

2.

Cut out and add a corbel to the bottom of each side. Glue to the castle where you think they should go.

NOW IT'S TIME! Cut up all the extra rubble (scrap paper), fill the walls, and put on the roofs.

Add more details. For example, use toothpicks as flag poles and/or string as a drawbridge chain.

RENDER

When most people hear the words "MEDIEVAL CASTLE" they imagine a very strong-looking, gray, stone-walled building. But, in fact, most castle walls were plastered over with what is called a lime render. This is a mixture of lime (not the fruit but the stone), sand, water, and something to hold it all together like animal fur. This was then applied like you would frost a cake. This render, after drying, not only gave a smooth appearance but also kept water out of the castle. This would wear away and need to be replaced fairly often and that is why we only see stone-wall castle ruins today. This render could also be painted with different colors of paint. As a matter of fact, medieval castles came in all colors. The reason for the colors was so the castle would stand out and could be seen far and wide showing dominance over its domain.

If you like your castle
with the stone wall
look, keep it as it is.

If you want to add a
render, pick a rad
poster paint color and
paint the castle as you
see fit.

EXTRA STONE IN CASE OF REPAIRS.

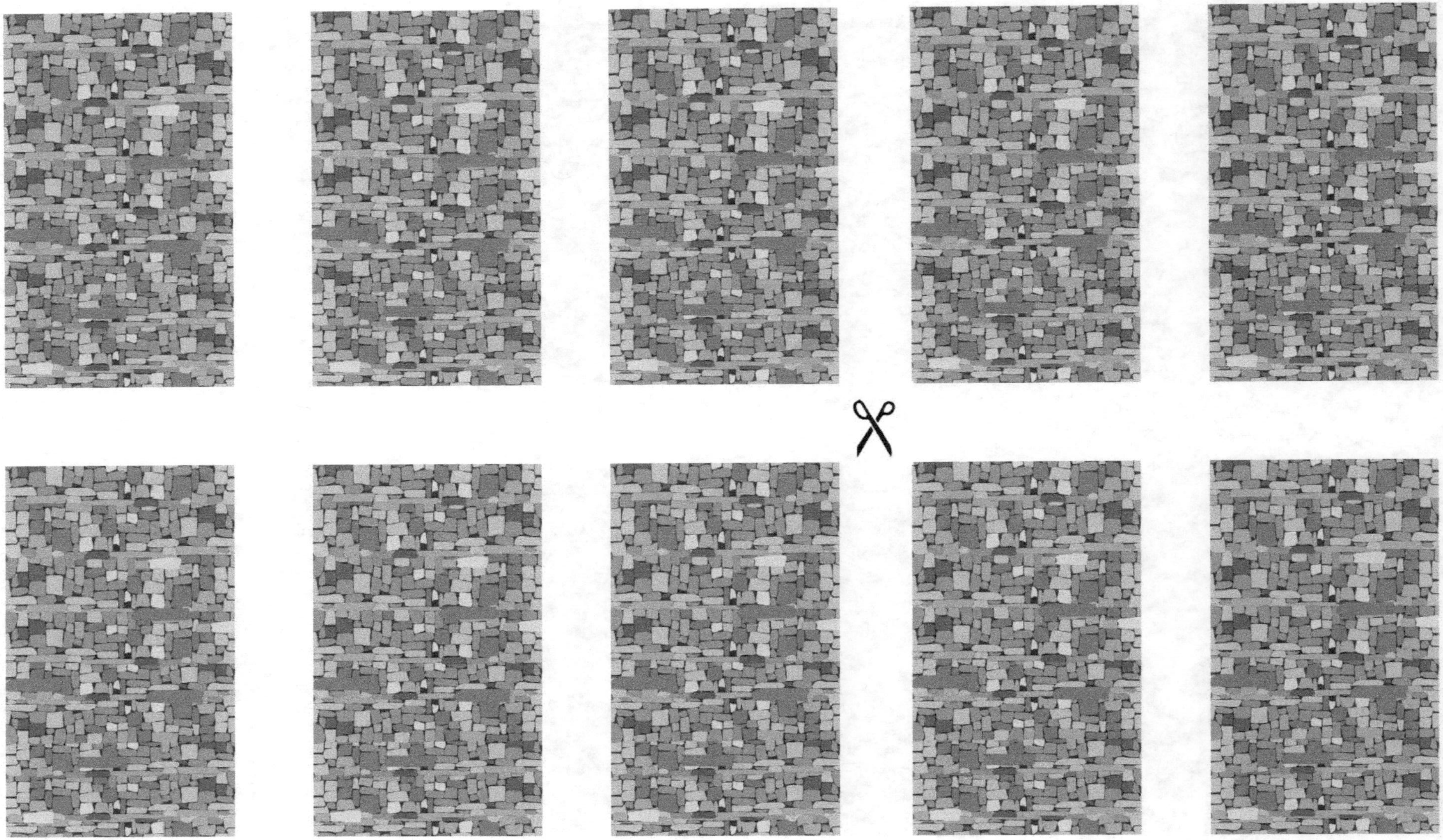

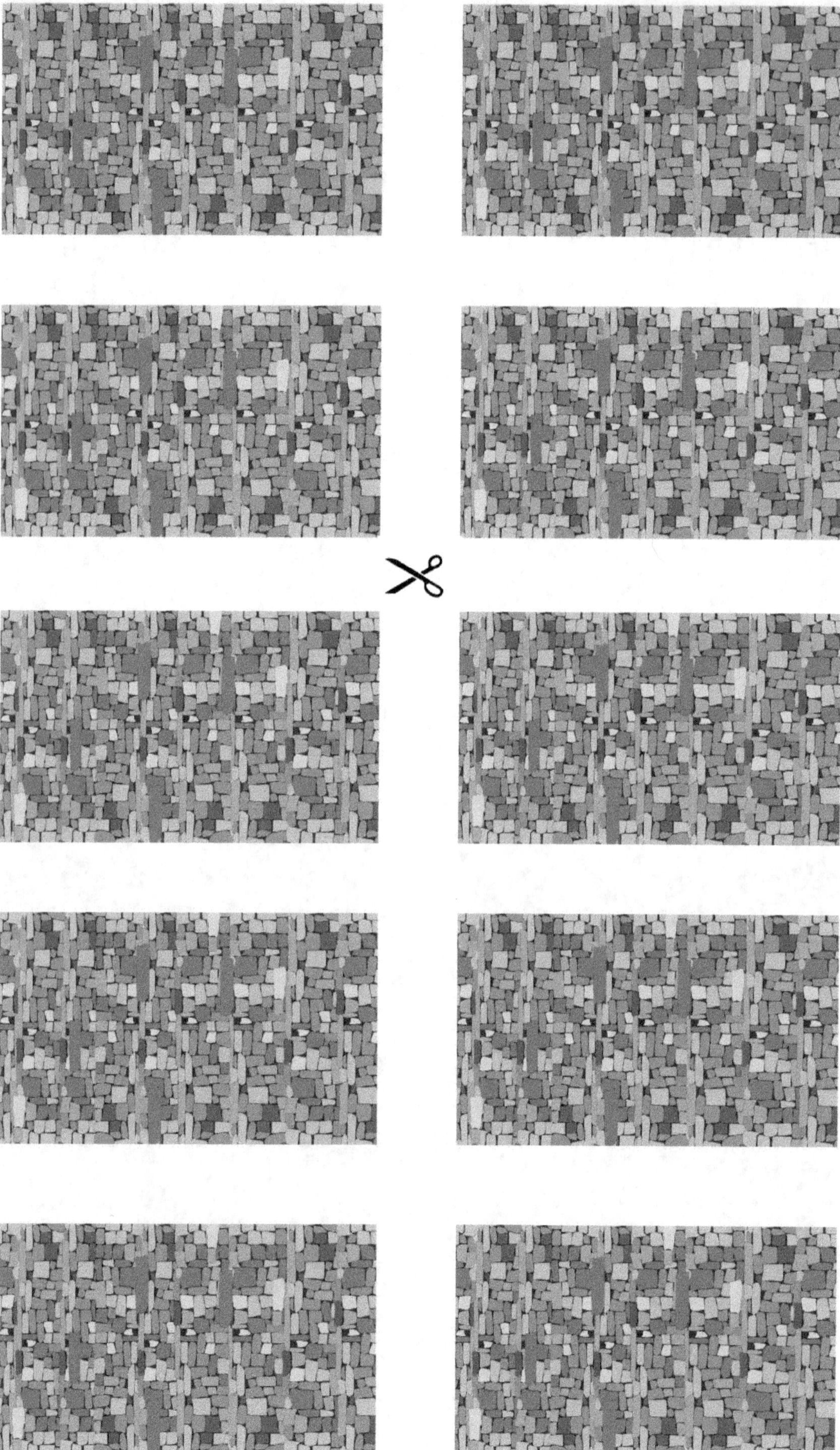

EXTRA STONE IN CASE OF REPAIRS.

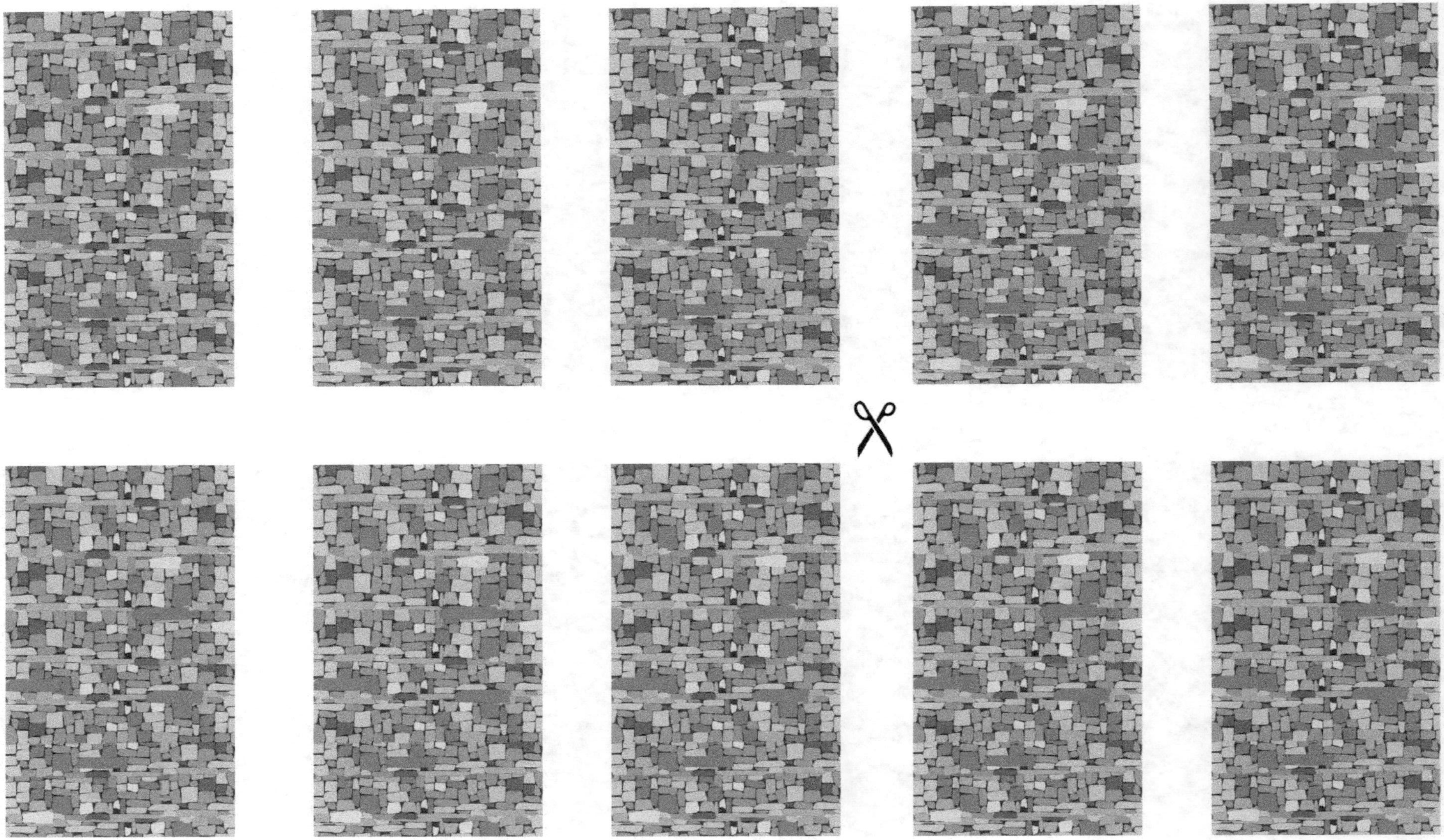

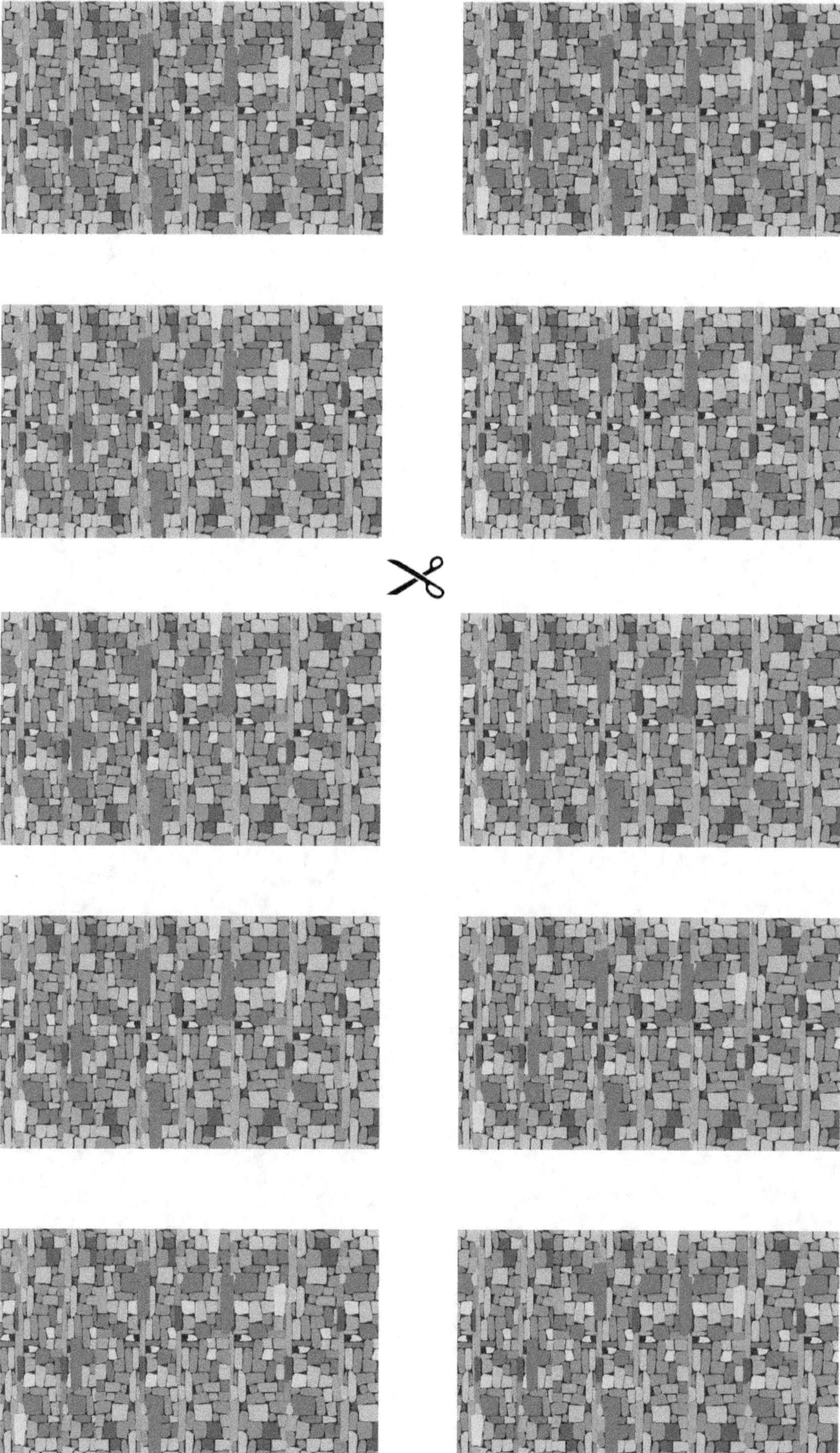

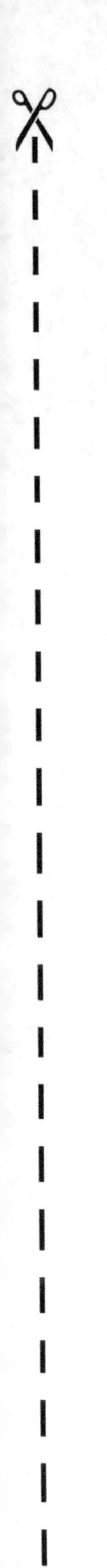

EXTRA STONE IN CASE OF REPAIRS.

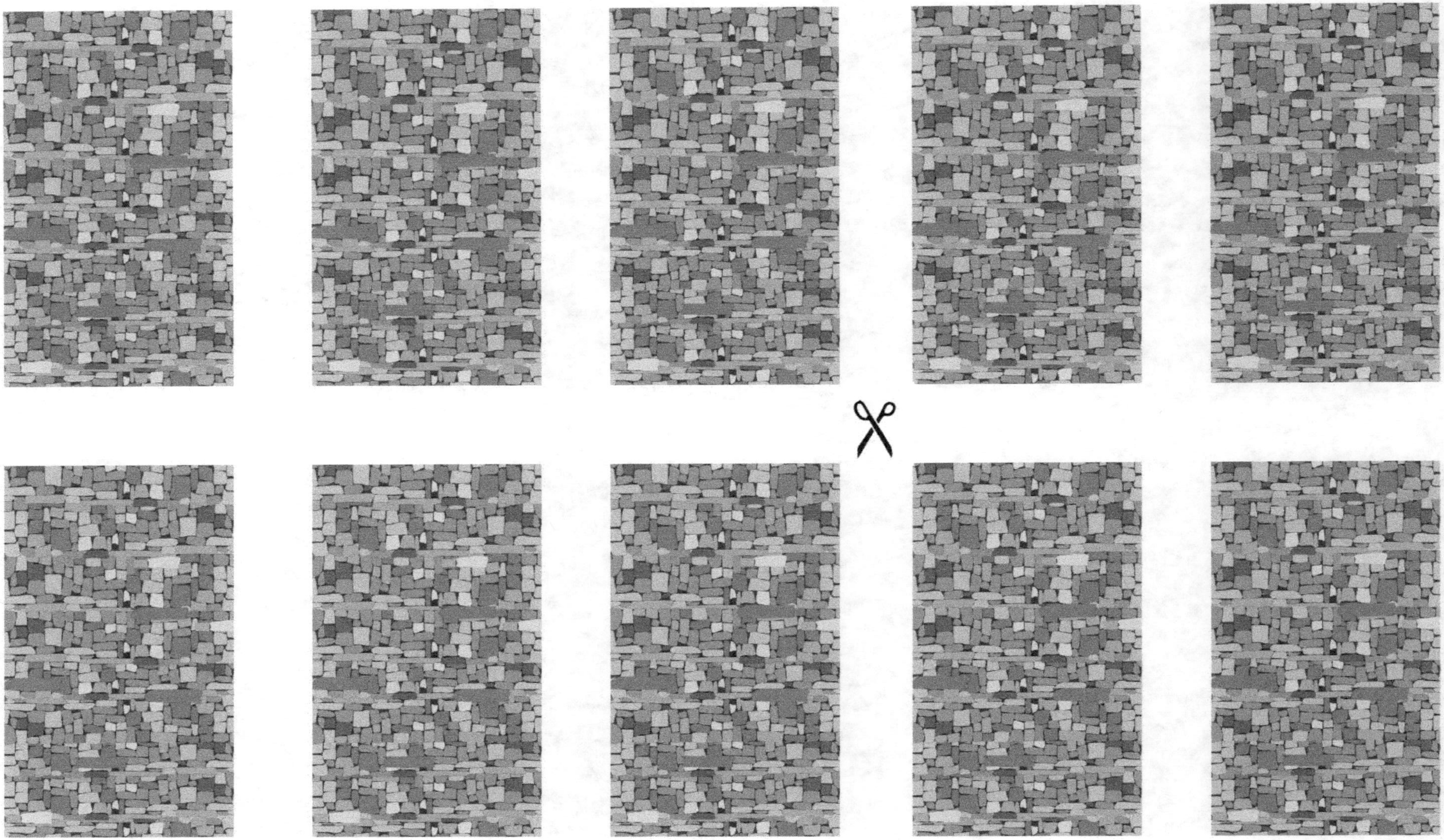

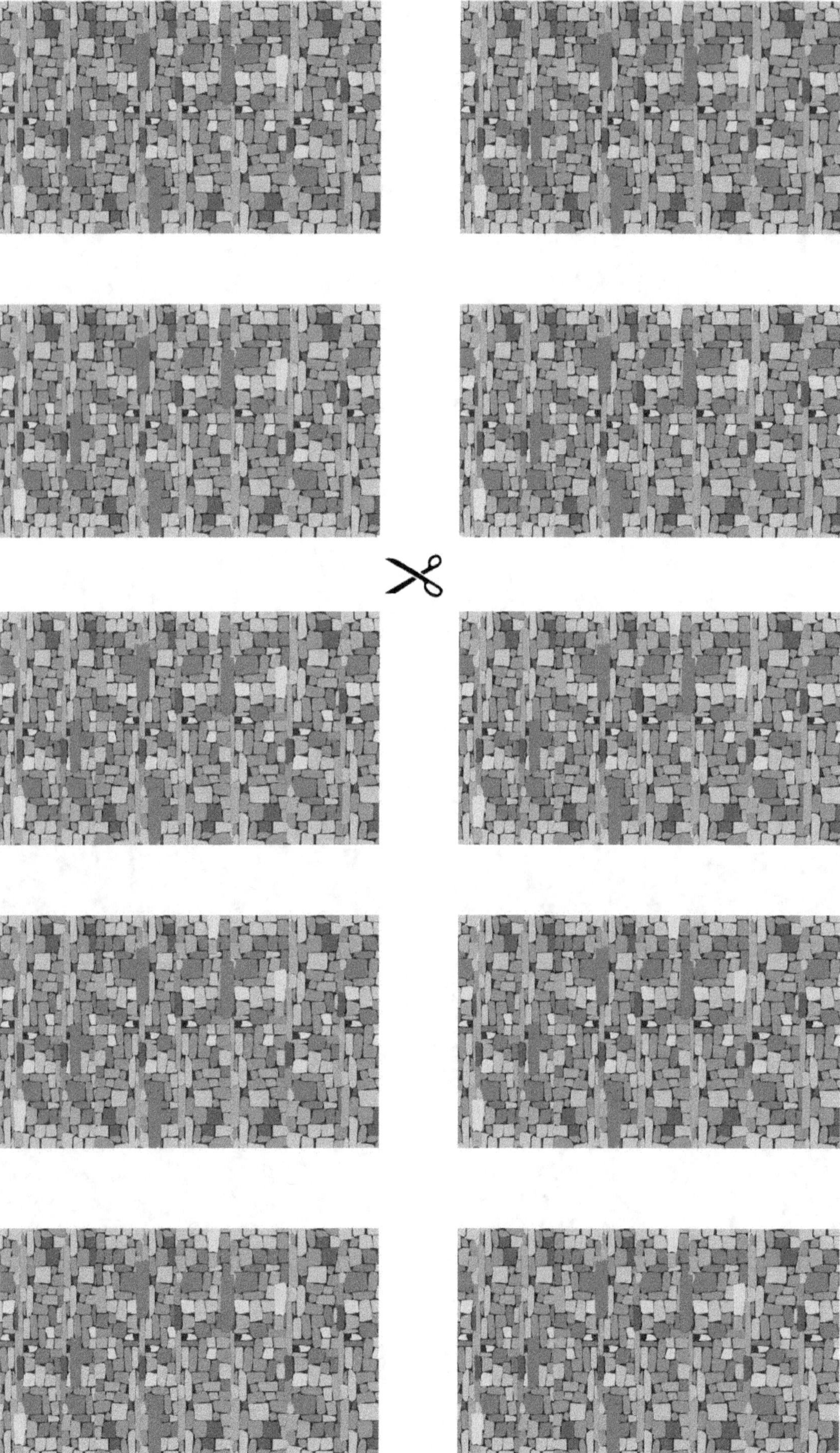

WELL DONE!

Congratulations castle builder on a great job building a medieval castle! Not only did you build a full-on castle with paper but you also learned some methods and techniques for what construction of a castle consisted of way back then in the old days. Your efforts have not gone unnoticed either. The Medieval Society of Supercilious Castle Builders has given you the Pickle Prize for "Awesome Castle Building". I hope you enjoyed all the activities in this book and if you like learning how stuff was/is built and designed and building paper models while you learn, check out some of the other books in my "How To Build" series. Until we meet again castle builder, Adios, Adieu, Avidazen, Anyong, Hasta La Vista, Signing out... I'm Albert B. Squid, SEE YAAAAAAAAAAAAAA!!!!!!!!!!!!!

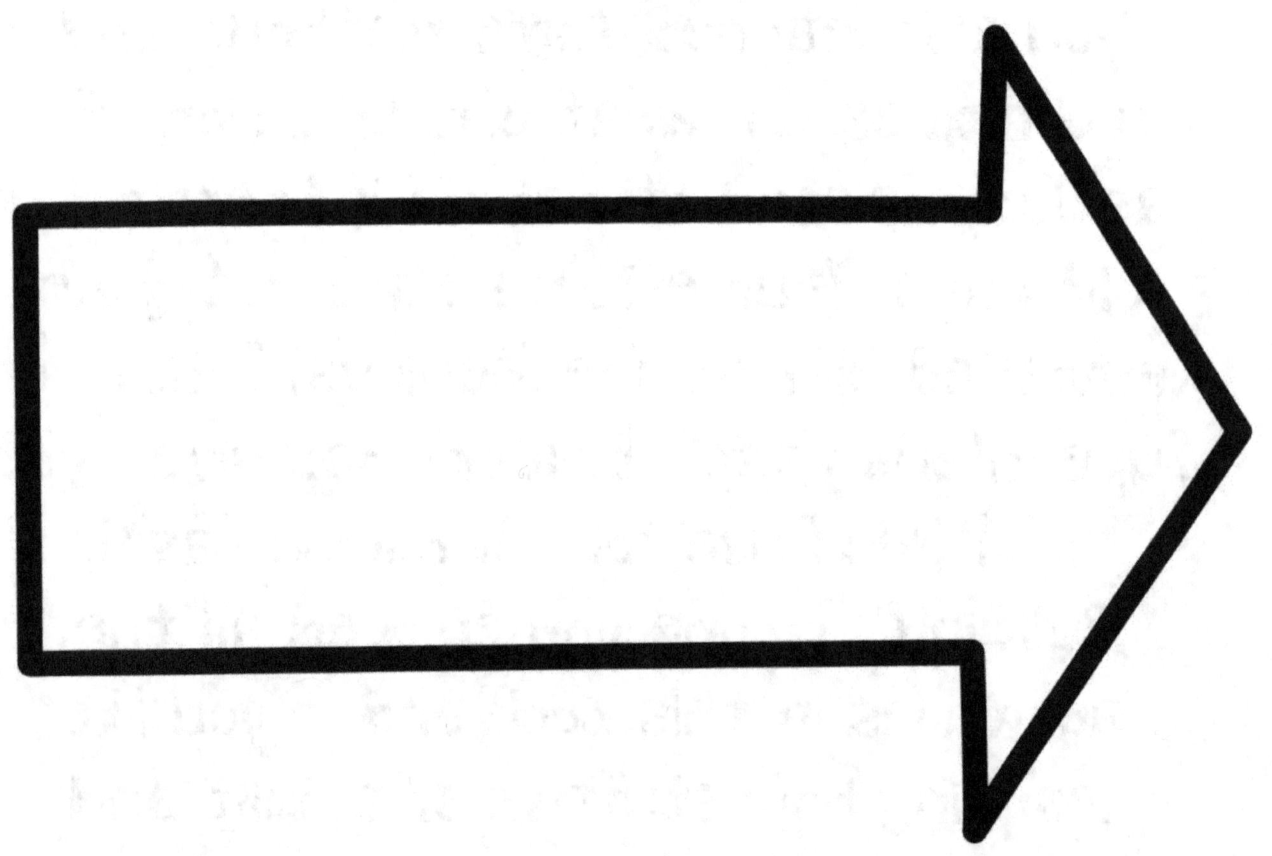

WE, THE MEDIEVAL SOCIETY OF SUPERCILIOUS CASTLE BUILDERS, GIVE YOU THIS AWARD

FOR EXCELLENCE IN CASTLE BUILDING SO YOU MAY CUT IT OUT AND HANG WHERE EVER YOU DESIRE.

PICKLE PRIZE FOR CASTLE BUILDING

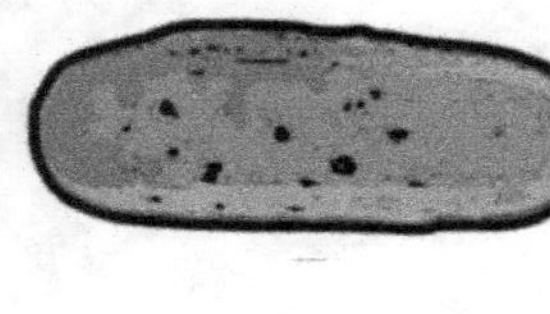

This is to certify that

____
(your name)

Has been bestowed the raddest of the rad, the coolest of the cool Pickle Prize in the order of medieval castle building and for their pursuit of knowledge in castle construction.

PROJECT NAME: _______________________________________

LOCATION: _______________________________________

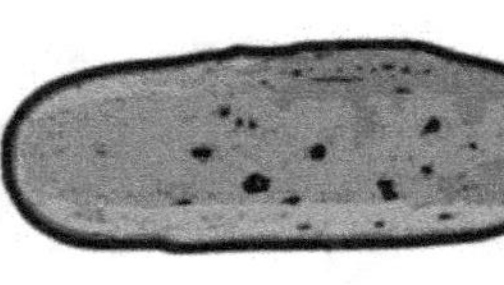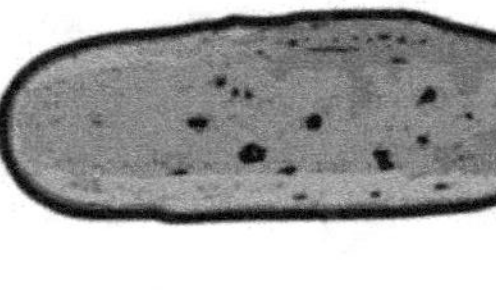

VERIFIED BY:_________________________   **DATE:**_______________

MORE BOOKS FROM THE SQUID

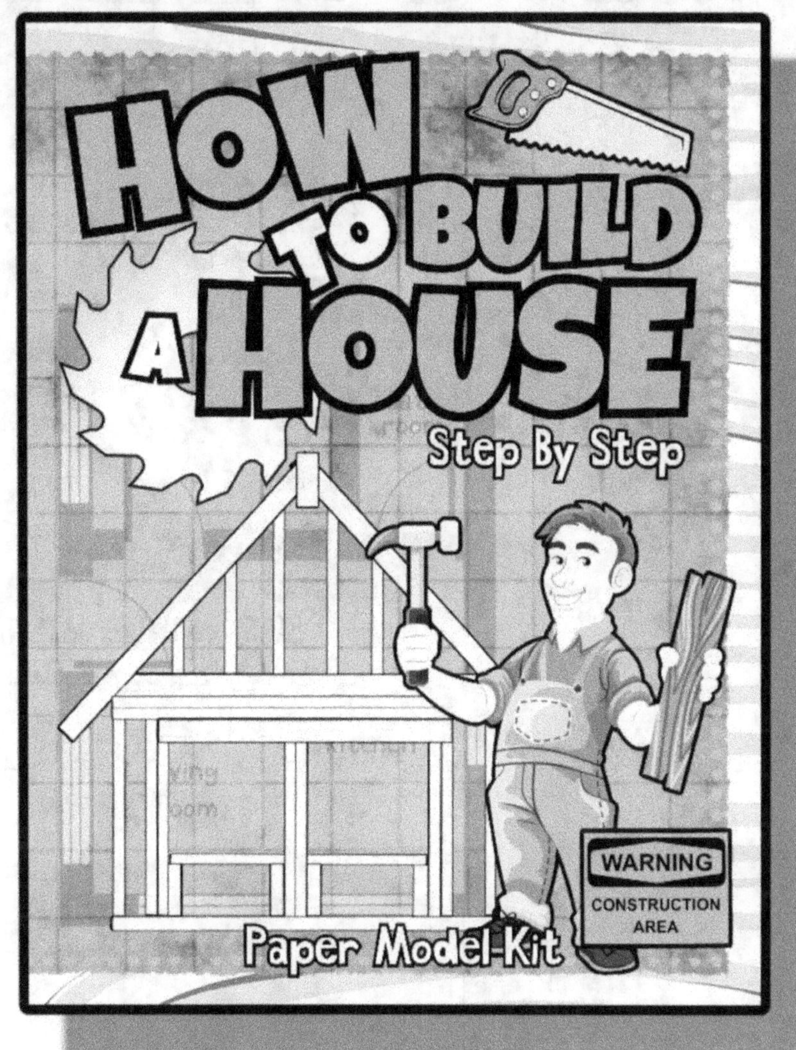

CHECK US OUT

ANSWER KEY

PAGE 23

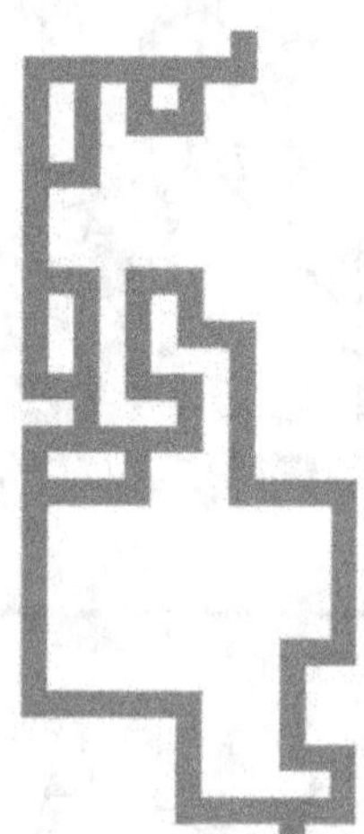

PAGE 24

PAGE 52

SIRE! IN THREE DAYS THERE
WILL BE A SIEGE!

PAGE 74

POSTERN
MOAT
BAILEY
KEEP
CURTAIN WALL

PAGE 38

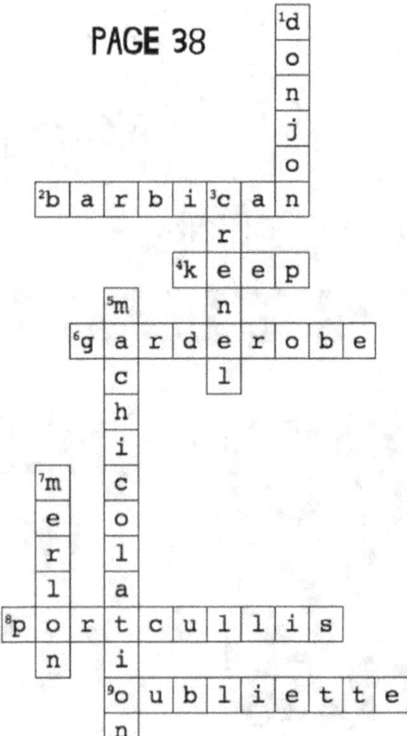

PAGE 73

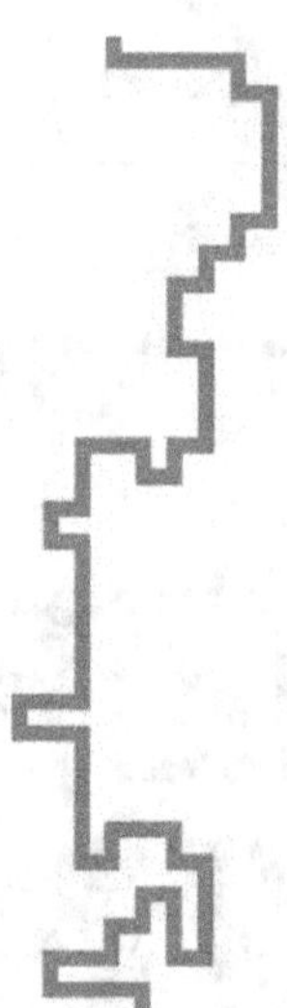

PAGE 78

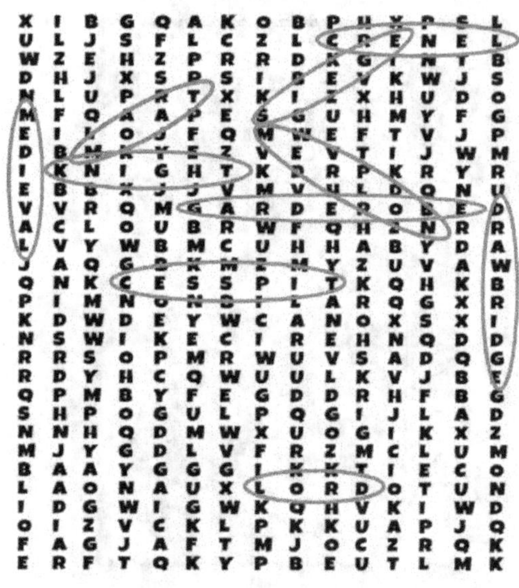

ABOUT THE AUTHOR

If you have a clue as to where Albert B. Squid might be, let us know at HQ by contacting us at:

info@squarerootofsquid.com

Born to a family of construction peeps, ALBERT B. SQUID was raised on construction sites in Massachusetts. Believe it or not, he holds two degrees in Engineering and Architecture and has worked as an Architect in Boston, Tokyo, and Seoul. In the year 2000, Squid started an independent children's book publishing company in NYC. I had fun doing that.....I mean HE (Albert B. Squid) had fun doing that! After becoming a freelance voice actor, the elusive author's whereabouts are unknown. He was last seen in Central Park in NYC wearing a gabardine suit and taking pictures of his pet pigeon named Teri Garfunkel with his bow tow which was really a camera.

NOTE: Although Squid likes to stay out of the public eye, he should be easy to spot with his hat with flaps, mirror sunglasses, and funny bow ties.

albertbsquid.com